Norfolk's best-selling magazine

First published in 2005 by Jarrold Publishing, Whitefriars, Norwich NR3 1JR
Telephone 01603 677318
www.jarrold-publishing.co.uk

Project Manager: Malcolm Crampton
Designer: Kaarin Wall
Editors: Nigel Haverson and Sally Whitman
Photographs supplied by Archant Regional Ltd, additional photography by Neil Jinkerson of Jarrold Publishing
Designed and produced by Jarrold Publishing
ISBN 0-7117-4180-8
Printed in Belgium 50723-1/05

EDITED BY

Neil Haverson

Introduction

Why do some stages of our lives evoke memories more than others? A spell in the services or playing for the village cricket team are sure-fire subjects to shoot yesterday's world into soft focus. And how we love to talk about the time our football team won the cup! But top of the list, surely, are schooldays. At *Let's Talk!* it is rare for our "memories" postbag not to contain a letter or photograph from a reader reminiscing about old school friends and favourite teachers – and wondering where they all are now.

Education has changed dramatically over the past 30 years. Gone are junior, secondary modern and most grammar schools. In their place we have first, middle and high schools. Desks are not in rows, students take calculators into exams, and the cane has been locked away for good.

Many of us treasure our days at school in the 50s and 60s where conkers and piggyback were common in the playground; where we walked sometimes miles to school without care or fear, and where teachers reigned supreme.

Those days are long gone but *Let's Talk!* has made sure they will never be forgotten. This affectionate look at education in an altogether gentler era will prompt memories of the days when you learned the three Rs, had a satchel rather than a backpack, and Turkey Twizzlers were light-years away from appearing on the school dinner menu.

As you journey through the days of short trousers, gymslips and school caps, you may spot someone you know.

Or even yourself!

Neil Haverson

Hands up! A typical classroom scene at Wymondham College in May 1965.

have high

John said,
"I like aeroplanes.
I want to go up in an aeroplane.
One day I shall have a ride
in a big aeroplane.
I shall go up high in an aeroplane."

12

her was

Janet sat in the sun.
Her doll was on her lap.
Mother was on the step.
"See what I have," said Mother.

13

The Contributors

Derek James grew up in Diss and went to Entry House School and then Earsham Hall School, near Bungay. Both closed after he left! He has worked on newspapers all over the country and is now features editor of the *Evening News* in Norwich.

Neil Haverson was born in Holt and has lived in Norfolk all his life. Educated at Hamond's Grammar School, Swaffham, he has worked for Archant, formerly Eastern Counties Newspapers, for 35 years. He is chief writer for *Let's Talk!* magazine.

Eric Read became an ARP warden in 1939 and was a member of the RAFVR from 1942 to 1964. He was a youth worker before taking up teaching. He taught at secondary schools in Norfolk. Now retired, Eric lives in Wymondham.

Colin Burleigh was born and grew up in Dereham. He went to Hamond's Grammar School, Swaffham, and worked for furniture manufacturers Jentique for 34 years. He is known as "Mr Jazz" for his long association with the Collegians Jazz Band.

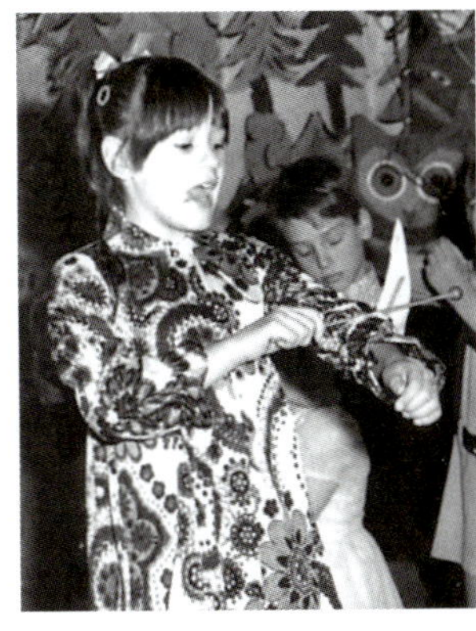

Margaret Haley comes from Wisbech but spent her childhood in Watton and Norwich. She attended Thetford Grammar School and the Blyth School in Norwich. Margaret became a teacher and taught at Wensum View, North Earlham and Catton Grove Schools.

Christine Townshend was born in Thetford and attended Norwich Road School before moving to the town's secondary modern. Christine, a keen supporter of Norwich City Football Club, still lives in South Norfolk and is Customer Service Manager for a housing association.

Juanita Hawkins from King's Lynn went to Terrington Marsh and West Winch primary schools before completing her education at Alderman Catleugh Secondary Modern School. She attended teacher-training college in Lincoln before teaching at various schools in King's Lynn.

Emma Delf lives in Carlton Colville near Lowestoft. Her schooldays were spent studying hard (and trying even harder to avoid PE) at the village primary school, Gisleham Middle School and Sir John Leman High School, Beccles. Emma is currently a member of the *Let's talk!* editorial team. She still avoids PE.

Infants and Juniors

What on earth is that? Children from Heather Avenue School, Hellesdon, wait expectantly at Bethel Street fire station in the 1960s.

Margaret Haley taught in Norwich schools in the 50s and 60s. She recalls a typical day and looks at how subjects were taught.

Younger children were not allowed pens; they were to use only pencils. Once they were old enough they could use pens with nibs, and then Biros. Pencil cases were brought from home and contained trigonometry equipment. Rulers and rubbers were provided by the school and rationed, so if a pupil lost any, they would have a black mark next to their name. All filled exercise books were kept and brought out for parents' and open days.

Parents' evenings were by appointments of 10 minutes each. This was when the truth came out about the pupil – this was the same as the dreaded reports, which were every term. Every subject was in black and white and was signed by the head. On open days there were displays of children's work.

There was a shortage of books; for example, one set for history was shared by three classes. The set was counted after the lesson to prevent loss. Lessons had to be arranged as to which class had the set of textbooks.

There was the annual visit of the school photographer. One by one the children were photographed and they watched in awe. It was an exciting day when a bundle of envelopes arrived and everyone saw everybody's photos (treasures to keep!).

Students: eight men at a time came from Morley College – quite a change for children, a break in normality.

In 1953 sweet rationing ended. No sweets were to be consumed in school. Girls stored half-consumed gob stoppers, bull's eyes, penny chews, barley sugar twists and humbugs in knicker pockets for the next convenient slot of legal consumption.

To raise school funds for Christmas party extras or outings, jumble sales took place. Money was also raised from waste paper.

Head teachers/teachers

Head teachers were very protective of staff. There was an incident involving me and a stringy 3rd-year child with thin, long blonde hair hanging over his eyes. On Friday afternoon, I took a Kirby grip and pinned his hair up so he could see to write. At 9am the next Monday, the head teacher summoned me to her room and said that the boy's father had brought her a letter threatening me with instant

Left A very busy playtime at Wroughton Junior School on the Gorleston Shrublands prefab estate in 1957. ***Right*** They won't bite! Children helping to feed Earlham Hall School's tame peacock and peahen in 1951.

dismissal by the Norfolk Education Council. The letter was so abusive that Miss Thomas fed it to the flames of her fire and said not to worry.

The relationship between child and teacher was close. A few confided in me about members of staff. It was unprofessional for me to listen, but unavoidable. I kept discipline easily, treating each child quite respectfully and expecting them to reciprocate, which they did. They were individuals.

Before extensive TV, children seemed more person-to-person with teachers. They quickly found out idiosyncrasies. For example one teacher used to say "shush" as a result of exhalation after almost every sentence so the children could not interrupt her. One child confided in me that the class counted 500 shushes in one lesson!

Discipline

Children were removed from class to stand outside if they behaved badly. If this happened, the child would hope that the head or deputy head would not pass by so there was no danger of being sent to

the head's room. Another discipline included losing one's playtimes and being made to write lines (and in several cases, lines to do at home). Some were kept in detention after school, but explanation had to be given to the parents. Sometimes parents were summoned to school. Unfinished work had to be finished in the pupils' own time by Friday afternoon. This was traumatic for the kids! Rewards were given for good behaviour and work, and there was also a star chart.

My own line, for a new class of about 50, was writing: "please, thank you and sorry" on the

A certain lapsed Roman Catholic spinster head teacher who loved The Sound of Music *made the whole school sit down in the hall and listen to the recording of it for the entire morning.*

blackboard and telling them they must use these a lot. Also, in the first hour, I would find out would-be hell-raisers and learn their names by repeating them. Personally, I had no problems with discipline; I treated my children with respect and honesty and I got the best back in return. I never sent a child home without sorting out differences. Otherwise I would wake up in the middle of the night and feel guilty in case they had an unhappy home.

It was possible to hug a child close while marking their work at the desk. Or comfort them on one's lap if distressed with a good old-fashioned cuddle. Now distance has to be maintained, which is a destroying factor in child–teacher relationships. Touch is very important to younger children, as with pets!

A headmistress in assembly would sometimes say: "Come out the badges!" These were the good ones who had won points for their team colour. It made us think of badgers crawling out!

The school day

8.50am *The school bell or whistle was sounded and the entire school lined up on the playground, divided into classes. The discipline was strict. In bad weather the children were allowed into the classrooms but early arrival was discouraged. The children had very basic cloakrooms, usually full of wet clothes and shoes. "Lost Property" was very common and was kept in a deposit until Friday when it was taken into the classrooms to find the owners. This led to a school rule of statutory labelling.*

There was a gradual introduction of uniform; it was generally worn by those who could afford it. Boys' uniform was a shirt, school tie, short trousers and a cap. Girls' uniform was a blouse, school tie and a navy or grey skirt. A different change of clothes was required for PT and dancing lessons; plimsolls were necessary. Those who had forgotten their PT uniform had to sit and watch.

9am *Registration. Those who were late were given*

What do you want to be when you grow up? Gaywood Primary School children in King's Lynn appeared rather overawed when they met the town mayor in 1965.

Left Hurry up, the bell's rung! The school at Hardingham in 1962.
Right Spring has sprung at a trip to Harford Hatcheries in Norwich, 1953.

an "L" in the register, and there was a black circle for absentees. Children had to read and learn spellings before going to assembly.
9.10am *Children went into assembly class by class, quietly and in good order. Assembly began with a hymn, followed by a religious reading or lecture from the head, then school affairs. It also included awards or reprimands specific to that day. Children were excluded from assembly on the grounds of different religious belief or if they had classroom jobs such as filling inkwells or giving out books.*
9.30am *The lessons began and were taught mainly through talking, and on the blackboard. There were some textbooks but these were well worn, especially the arithmetic ones, which were counted very carefully. Arithmetic lessons consisted of chanting 2 times to 12 times tables, oral tests, and teaching the rules of addition, subtraction, multiplication and division. Slim notebooks were used for weekly written tests. Children were given squared exercise books for all written work, which was marked carefully by the teachers. Corrections had to be done and, in the 60s, those who were able were allowed to work through the textbook at their own pace.*
10.25am *The lesson came to an end and all the books were cleared away as the children went out*

to play for 15 minutes. Toys and games included hoops, skipping ropes, whips and tops, hopscotch (marked on the ground) and children making up their own games. "Free arms" was a game of catch. One child was nominated to do the chasing, and then children who were touched had to stand still until another child freed them by touching them. The last free child then became the chaser.

Another game was "chains". The nominated child had to catch another child and become a chain. This would continue until a huge chain of children was running around the playground. The discipline was very strict so there was no bullying. Later in the 60s, some school equipment was provided for playtimes, such as different sized balls and skipping ropes. They were carefully counted after playtime. Other toys and games included yo-yos, cap guns, cat's cradle and conkers when in season. Playgrounds were very bleak – there was no place for hide-and-seek – and very few places had a school field (grass). In bad weather, break and lunchtime were spent inside, in the classroom. Games included old comics such as Dandy, Beano, *disused books,* Tiny Tots *and children's own board games.*

11.40am *After break time children had English for an hour and a half until lunch time. English was taught through talking and on the blackboard. Grammar, punctuation, spelling and reading were all taught in groups, each with an able leader. The 'look and see' and phonic methods were used (*Janet and John*-style group readers). Compositions such as "My family" and "My favourite day of the week" were completed. Poetry was a big feature, as*

These smartly dressed children are particularly proud of their harvest display at Dell Primary School, Lowestoft, in autumn, 1966.

Royal

Left The headmaster from St Edmunds Junior School, King's Lynn, is raised into the air on a visit to a nearby fire station in 1972 – much to the amusement of the children.

Right These Great Yarmouth girls put their playtime to constructive use making daisy chains, 1962.

was speaking aloud. Weekly writing lessons were taught from the blackboard. Poems, spellings and exercises were copied into exercise books from the blackboard, initially in print and then written in cursive handwriting. This helped the children to understand and learn capital letters. The alphabet would be chanted and sung, as it was very important to know your ABC for the 11-Plus tests.

12.15 to 1.50pm *Lunch time. School meals were eaten in the canteen and were two courses: main, usually made up of peas, pie and potatoes, and a dessert. Mashed potatoes, beefburgers and sausages were common, as were fish and chips every Friday. Dessert was usually steamed sponge with custard or rice and prunes. Lucky children were allowed seconds – nothing was ever wasted. Some children brought in packed lunches. In the lunch hour, there was a lot of hard work done by the teachers in order to prepare for lessons.*

After lunch *PE lessons were usually once a week.*

Children were initially taught about shillings and pence with cardboard coins. To help with the learning of money, children collected things from home such as cartons and tins to make shops. The classroom had a pair of scales and weights to teach pounds and ounces. Each child had a wooden ruler and wall charts to measure heights.

They were held mainly in the school hall when the weather was bad and on the playground in good weather. Schools that did not have a games field had to have a supervised walk to the nearest one. Hoops were used in PT for skipping, twisting around the body (waist and arm), bowling and balancing. Ropes were also used – one child wriggled it while the other jumped over it – as were balls and bats. In the 60s netball posts and markings on the playground were introduced. Apart from this, there was not much equipment; wall bars did not arrive till later. To warm up, the teacher would take the whole class and demonstrate bending and stretching: "Tall as a house, small as a mouse". Rowing boats and hopping like rabbits was especially for younger children. The class was divided into groups of red, blue, yellow and green, each wearing their team-colour bands. One of the team games was the first team to get all its members to finish the race and sit down with their hands on their heads. Team points were awarded, so the games were very competitive. Each team took turns in playing with ropes, hoops and balls. Dancing also took place once a week. Boys were encouraged to join in and they did! The teacher played on the piano while the children danced. The songs played were 78 records: folk dances such as "Galopede" (danced in sets), "Haste to the Wedding", "Bonnets so Blue" and "Circassion" circle. This super dance was when the whole hall was used for the children to create a big circle and dance to "Turning the

Left The school run was causing problems as long ago as 1970. Parents deliver their children to Little Plumstead School on the first day back after the summer holidays. ***Right*** Parents and pupils pick their way over a muddy school route to Caister Infant School in 1966. Mums and dads had previously threatened to keep their children away from the school if nothing was done about the condition of the footpath.

Enthusiastic beginners give it their all at the opening of the Alderman Catleugh School, King's Lynn swimming pool in July 1965. The school's PE master at the time offered to run beginners classes for parents too!

Stocking" played on the piano. The BBC broadcast was also danced to for 20 minutes. A lot of exercise was gained through walking to school.

The afternoon lessons were usually more relaxed and included subjects such as nature study, geography, history, handwork, arts and crafts; the BBC broadcast provided a 20-minute slot on certain subjects. This was very popular and a welcome relief all round. It was also used for one assembly a week.

Arts and crafts *The lessons were making things from cost-free objects. One example was to cover egg boxes with tiny pieces of screwed-up coloured crepe and tissue paper, using paste to form Easter presents for family members (to put eggs in). The school paste was powder mixed with water and placed in jam jars. After a while it smelt bad and turned a brownish colour on top. One 3rd-year boy in Mr Prince's class actually relieved himself in the jar that was permanently on the teacher's desk. The boy became a kind of hero! Children were encouraged to bring in anything useful such as toilet rolls, boxes, wallpaper, jam jars, old wool and pieces of material. They were used to construct anything from houses to trains to knitted squares to make a communal blanket. There was a lot of knitting for girls, ring-making for boys and French tatting (four nails in top of cotton reel to weave wool in and out, to make a long chain) which was stuck in a circular fashion on a cardboard base to make a tablemat. There was a lot of paper work. To make frames newspapers were cut into*

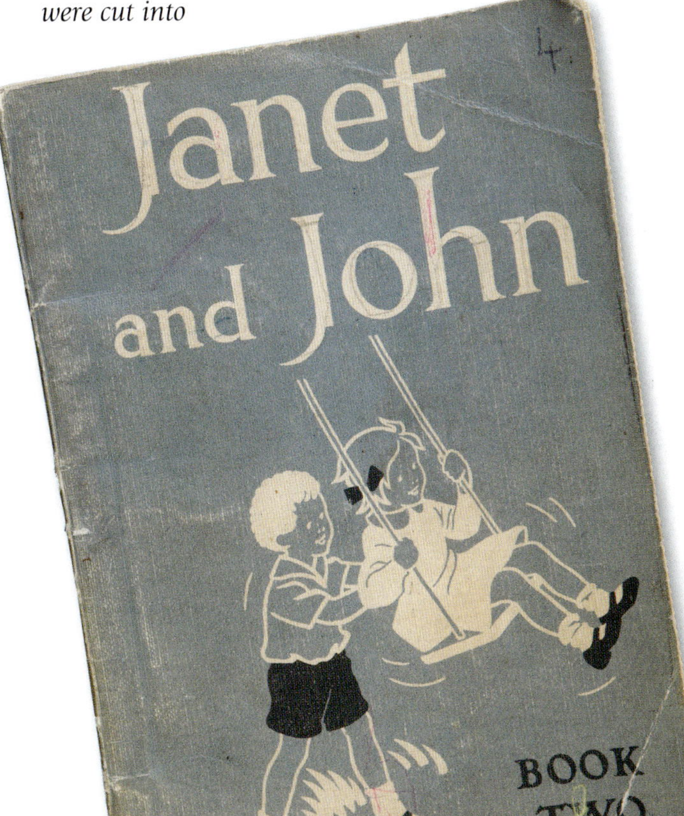

Left A peaceful scene at the school in Aylsham, winter 1957. *Right* Which page are we on? Christmas carols at Brandon School in 1966.

strips, coloured in and then weaved into each other. Coloured squares, matchboxes and paperclips were used to make a chest of drawers, and jars were decorated with screwed-up paper. Cards were always handmade for every occasion and the game snakes and ladders was made from using coloured paper and buttons for counters. Papier-mâché was used to make little bowls which were then painted. It was messy but fun!

Art *Children were sometimes allowed to draw and colour in pictures of what they liked. One boy proudly drew the inside of a slaughterhouse! There was a lot of freedom in art. Children also sketched anything they found in the school fields. They also drew each other. Collages made up of different items such as toffee papers and labels were created to depict current and historical events, and used for geography topics.*

Drama *This was fun for the children. It was mainly acting plays in class but dressing up was included. The children also had to collect dressing-up clothes from home.*

Friday afternoons *These were a time of joy. There were games on the field for the 4th-years. There was "own choice" or "choosing time" before afternoon play. Children could bring in their own toys, dolls or toy cars to show each other. After playtime there was story time for younger children when the teacher would read aloud a story to finish the week. Some children chose to work. A large dressing-up box with discarded clothes and jewellery was available. This was a huge fun thing, especially with the very young. There was a box of tattered old comics which was brought out for wet lunch times. Jigsaws were also available but there was much frustration with missing pieces. Simple charades and "I Spy" were also played as a class.*

A male teacher was giving an elderly spinster school-teacher a lift home. When the teacher braked sharply, glossy magazine pages full of ladies in their underwear flew forward from under the passenger seat into the foot-well! In an effort to explain, he said he had to remove these pages so the children would not see them when they used old magazines to cover the table.

Geography *Based on tracing maps from old atlases, this was fun for the children. A model of the British Isles was made out of papier-mâché; this was used to learn about mountains. On Gala Day, each class was donated a globe.*

Nature study *This was a lot of fun for the children. They would leave the classroom to go and see what they could find on the school field. The process followed was identify, label, and then discuss. There was a lot of sketching and note taking involved. Things identified were collections of wild flowers, which were kept in jam jars; collections of leaves (when in season); all trees, birds and creatures. Broad beans were grown in jam jars, and wormeries were constructed. The children learned about the seasons and the importance of bird's nests and hibernation. Footprints in the snow were also studied. Caterpillars were kept in jars with their special food; cabbage and ragwort for moths. The top of each jar was made from pierced paper so that the creatures could breathe, but it was also often an escape route!*

History *A lot of time was spent copying pictures and pages of writing from textbooks. The 1st-years worked on the Stone Age to the Romans while 4th-years got to work on World War One.*

Earlham Hall School, autumn 1950: these youngsters are totally absorbed by what their teacher has to say.

The charming world of childhood fantasy was vividly captured in this model depicting nursery rhyme scenes, a gift to Diss Church Infant School in January 1953 from an American lieutenant who was an artist in civilian life.

Music *Lessons consisted of everybody playing (and owning) a recorder. The school orchestra played once a week in assembly. Percussion bands were also fun. Music was folksy in the 50s and 60s. There was always one music enthusiast teacher who used up a lot of lesson time which disadvantaged the three Rs. School choirs were not very demanding.*

Homework *The amount given depended on the teacher. Homework was usually spelling, learning words and knowing the 2 to 12 times table.*

When I go shopping, I often get recognised by staff and ex-pupils and am expected to remember all the names! One lady confessed to me that when she was younger she stole £1 off my desk. We laughed and her son asked if she paid it back. I said no!

Attitudes of children

The children were basically nice, and bad language or bullying was very unusual. There was much respect for teachers. Children liked to be chosen as monitors to do special jobs and liked to be put in charge. Examples included putting straws in milk and ink in wells, tidying books and being paint monitors. Some children preferred to do jobs in the classroom at playtime and in lunch hours. For swearing – and this could include using phrases like "stocking tops" or "district nurse" – they were sent out of the classroom to wash their mouths out with soap. Gifts were given to the teacher: an eight-year-old red-head who used to tell me that her mother had a different daddy in bed every morning brought me jam tarts for my lunch – disposed of discreetly! Flowers were sometimes brought for the teacher: I used to get wonderful bunches at Wensum View School but I discovered they had originated from the Jewish cemetery on Bowthorpe Road! Children loved being helpful by collecting things like jam jars for school use.

Children of all ages then and now feel their way with adults. In the days before the media started bombarding them with distractions and adult propaganda there was a genuine

Is that a dragon or a large dog? Shipdham Primary School concert in the spring of 1976.

innocence among children curious about adult life. Children's attitude to adults and teachers was that they had respect – even fairy-tale fantasies about the person they were involved with for a large percentage of their everyday life. Personally, I am still proud to be involved with many of my ex-pupils and their families from the 50s and 60s. The answer is friendliness and mutual trust. Children were appreciative – a former pupil of mine said, "I didn't listen to what you were saying but used to love watching you!"

Class division

Classes were divided into groups A, B, C and D academically, A being the most able. This was not good for the lower groups as they were made to feel quite inferior early in life. For a teacher to be given the C and D groups was quite a challenge – even though the more able children actually needed more handling. These children were said to be "streamed" into different abilities. When mixed ability came into fashion, primary school children were streamed for the three Rs, especially in arithmetic. Streaming was very beneficial because the more able children were not held back in mixed ability classes.

School furniture

In the 60s the ghastly desks, including teachers' desks, were updated, which brought great joy. It also became fashionable to have groups of tables and chairs instead of regimented rows of double desks. Some teachers preferred the lines but the children liked the new "grouping" desks. It made it easier for the teachers to designate groups of children of varying ability for reading etc. With tables, however, the class had to have a locker each for storing their books. This was not as compact as having storage in a desk.

Cloakrooms and toilets were medieval and basic. They were unpleasant due to the presence all day of wet clothes and outdoor shoes. Nobody lingered in them!

Accidents in class plays were very funny! Humpty Dumpty once lost his head, which was originally a box!

Life at a tiny village school was very different from being educated in a town or city. Juanita Hawkins, nee Bolt, attended Terrington Marsh County Primary School. She describes life at a school where space was at a premium.

Terrington Marsh County Primary School was originally a one-roomed brick building, built, I would think, in Victorian times. By the time I started school in 1968 there was also a green wood and galvanised iron extension which housed the infants. There were sinks in the infant cloakroom for washing hands before dinner and before beginning the weekly needlework lesson (girls only). The toilets were outside at the bottom of the playground, a nuisance to get to in bad weather but at least they were flushing ones! The urinal part of the boys' toilets was just a wall and sometimes we girls would dare each other to peep round it!

The teaching staff was a husband-and-wife-team, Mr and Mrs Wilde. Most of the time Mr Wilde, who was the head teacher, taught juniors and his wife taught infants. Once a week, however, the boys would trot off to the juniors' room to learn woodwork with Mr Wilde, whilst the girls would go to the infants' room to do needlework with Mrs Wilde. The first things we attempted to sew were on the fabric with large holes known as "binca". Mrs Wilde had a large piece of binca with lots of examples of stitches and patterns on, and we would choose one at a time to copy. Later we moved on to making such things as handkerchiefs, small stuffed toys and a doll's cot cover. I made a little horse from green gingham with plaited wool for the tail.

Touch one, I dare you! Roman Hill School children in Lowestoft pictured during a tour of the quayside as part of their lessons on the fishing industry, October 1970.

BIRDS EYE

At lunch times Mrs Collison, who was dinner lady, caretaker and cleaner, came to look after us. She dished out the hot dinner, which had been cooked elsewhere, and then came to the playground with us. I remember being told off for stirring the jam into my rice pudding, then looking up to see Mrs Wilde doing exactly the same thing! How we remember such injustices, even after all these years! I also remember a pie made with minced pork and decorated with a little raised circle of pastry: we called it belly-button pie, and tried to convince the younger ones that that was what it was really made of!

At lunch times Mrs Collison would play games with the younger ones. There was "I sent a letter to my love", "Ring a ring of roses", "Farmer's in his den", or "B-I-N-G-O" and, if you fell over and hurt your knee, one rub with her "magic finger" would stop the tears. The very first lesson I remember in the infants' class is learning the letter "e". Mrs Wilde wrote it on my little chalkboard, demonstrating that if you continued it you would get an egg in an egg cup. I spent ages going over and over it with different coloured chalks – though I doubt very much if it still looked like the right shape when I'd finished!

At that time the latest method of learning to read was something called ITA, the initial teaching alphabet. This tried to overcome the difficulties of the same letters having different sounds, e.g. "o" in "old", and "hot", by having different symbols for each sound – "hot" but "oeld". I remember reading about Sally and Paul who liked ice-cream: I wonder what happened to all those books when ITA fell out of fashion because of the problems it caused when pupils tried to spell. I still have an ITA book

Come on, it's not that deep! Children wait for others to cross as they make their way to school at a flooded Bawburgh.

One teacher chose two children to carry a blackboard full of writing and follow him around the school – he himself carried the books. His advice to me as a new girl was "never be seen without carrying books and preferably followed by two children carrying a board covered in writing"!

Encouragement and excitement on these faces at the Gaywood Primary School sports day in June 1972.

called The Oeld Man and the Bird, *given to me one prize-giving – it caused much hilarity when I showed it to my fellow students at teacher-training college! My cousin Sharon, who is the same age as me, had another ITA book –* Little O's Naughty Day; *naturally, I thought her book was much better!*

Maths was taught mainly around the four rules of number (+, –, X, ÷). In the infants' class we used a set of cards with bright pictures at the top, which teacher had made and stored in green gingham pockets. I remember my pride at having completed all of these, causing Mrs Wilde to write the sums directly in my book. As well as bright plastic counters, we used the brand new unifix cubes for counting – I would fight to get the maroon-coloured ones and, as I tell my pupils now, I would be told that it really didn't matter what colour they were as they were just for counting!

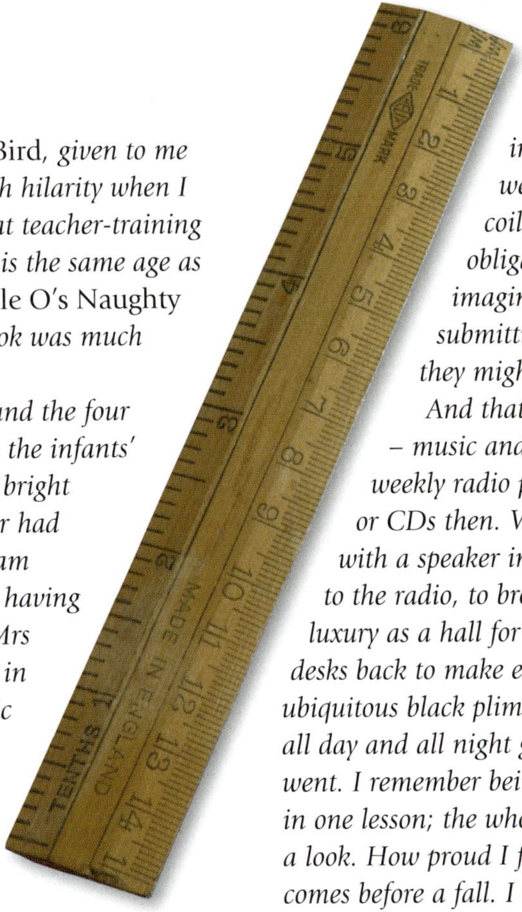

At morning play we would each have our little bottle of milk which, in the winter, would often be frozen, the cream having pushed the foil lid up an inch or so. In the afternoons we would get out the colourful, coiled rush mats to have the obligatory afternoon rest. I can't imagine the infants I teach now submitting to that, although I think they might benefit from it!

And that favourite of all lessons – music and movement. This was a weekly radio programme, no cassette tapes or CDs then. We had this big wooden box with a speaker in it, presumably connected to the radio, to broadcast it. Having no such luxury as a hall for PE, we simply pushed the desks back to make enough room and donned the ubiquitous black plimsolls. I would have worn mine all day and all night given the chance! And off we went. I remember being praised for my bunny hops in one lesson; the whole class was stopped to have a look. How proud I felt! Well, as they say, pride comes before a fall. I was so proud that I began to show off by kicking higher and higher, ending by flipping over right on to my back, to my great embarrassment!

The day always finished with a good old-fashioned story time. As we gathered around

teacher's desk on our little wooden chairs, she would read to us from her collection out of the teacher's lovely old wooden cupboard. My favourite was always Dorothy Edwards' Naughty Little Sister *stories. I would hold my breath in anticipation of the feared punishment she would receive for all her naughtiness. You might like to know that infant children still enjoy those stories today!*

What a pity that so many of these little schools have now closed! I understand all the economic arguments, and the demands of today's National Curriculum would certainly place a great burden on just two teachers, but I do feel children today miss out on the great family feeling that such small schools engendered.

I still remember the feeling of great pride when I stepped through the adjoining door to the junior class of my little two-roomed school. I was especially proud because it had been decided that I was ready for this great day in my last term as an infant, instead of waiting for the new school year to begin in September.

Of course I was already familiar with the room as the place where daily morning assembly was held. Three days a week Mr Wilde, the head teacher, would lead the assembly while Mrs Wilde, his wife, would play the piano. We used the With Cheerful Voice *hymn book, which had a groovy pink and purple wavy pattern on the cover. Once a week we listened to the BBC radio service. I remember the hymn book for it was sky blue with an orange sun rising. We sang the usual hymns like "All things bright and beautiful" and "Loving shepherd of Thy sheep". I was uplifted by the majesty of the tune to "Hills of the north rejoice" and always thrown by the chorus of "Lift up your hearts", which somehow didn't follow the direction I expected!*

Left Intense concentration under the watchful eye of the teacher at the school in Oulton, 1974.

Right The cast of the 1965 Mulbarton School nativity play take it all very seriously.

No more sticky-backed plastic for us! The 38 pupils of class three proudly show off their Blue Peter badges in the infants department of West Lynn School., March 1974. The class were awarded the prized possessions after they wrote to the programme as part of a class project.

Every Friday, instead of the usual assembly, the teachers had a break while the more senior children took charge of "the Good Samaritan Club". We brought pennies to save in the empty dried milk tin for charity (and we collected silver foil for Guide Dogs for the Blind too). A major part of it was chanting the story of the Good Samaritan together. I remember near the end it was "and – brought – him – to – an – inn – and – took – care – of – him". Of course some would take advantage of the situation and misbehave.. The punishment for this was to stand at the front with your hands on your head till released. If things got really bad then Mr and Mrs Wilde would have to be called in. Nobody wanted this because then we would have to start lessons!

We sat in pairs at wooden desks with lift-up lids and holes for inkwells, though we used Biro pens or pencils rather than ink pens. Inside, the desks had a little hole in the corner which was very useful for pushing out dirt into the bin at the end of term! Our chairs were single wooden ones. All desks faced the front of course, though Mr Wilde's big desk was to one side. The blackboard was a large rollaway one on wheels so it could be moved around the room as necessary.

By the time we reached the juniors we were weaned off ITA reading books and enjoyed the delights of Wide Range Readers, blue and green series. In those days reading books were never taken home as they are today; learning was something that happened at school, taught by teachers, not something parents did. We also had a choice of library books in the magnificent glass-fronted bookcases; these were changed periodically when the library van visited.

English was taught using the Ronald Ridout workbooks. (Good old Ronald – he must have written hundreds of educational books in his time.) These books were about A4 size and had dull grey covers. However, the first instructions in them, apart from writing your name, was to decorate the front cover. I could have taken several lessons to do this if only I was allowed!

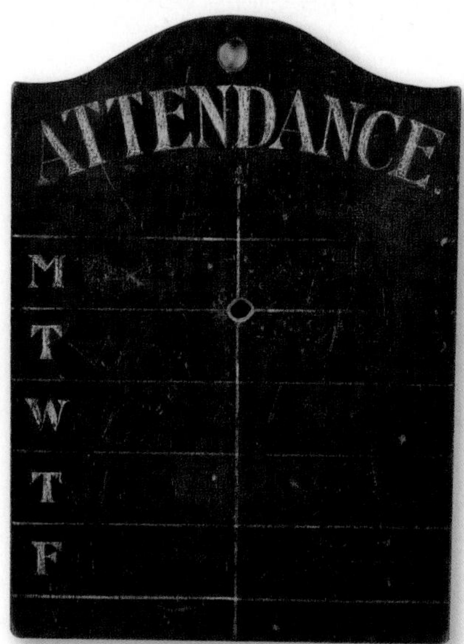

We had flat tins of Derwent pencil crayons for everyday work – the sky blue was my favourite – and Golden Virginia tobacco tins of wax crayons for wet playtimes. The tin that had the small bright red and the thick white crayons was my favourite. I would open each tin before choosing, much to the annoyance of the teachers!

Maths was taught from the pink Alpha *and blue* Beta *books. Again I remember my pride at being put on the* Beta *book because I had finished the* Alpha *one. Counting apparatus included Cuisenaire rods which definitely helped me learn my number bonds of ten. These were wooden rods of varying sizes and colours, coded to match their length in centimetres – the 'ones' were natural wood, the 'twos' were a bright pink, and the 'tens' were orange. As it was in the early 70s the decimal system was brand new, and we used cardboard decimal coins, rulers with both inches and centimetres, and thermometers in centigrade. I don't remember any of the science, geography or history we must have learned, though our friend Ronald Ridout wrote the history textbooks. (Why on earth do I remember his name so vividly? Perhaps it's the alliteration of those two Rs?) I think most of our science was nature study, like pressing and naming wild flowers. I remember a project on birds and the sheer frustration at not being able to draw a swallow's tail properly – it looked more like it was wearing trousers which were falling down!*

One of my favourite lessons was country dancing. Having no hall, we simply pushed the desks back to make room and put on our plimsolls. How I loved skipping round with my partner, singing to "The Blaydon Races", forming stars of four people; the exciting scrum of "Stirring Up The Dumplings"; the "Cumberland Reel" and best of all "Lucky Seven". This last dance was very tricky at first, needing you to kind of shake hands with seven people, one after another, until you swung round with the last one. One dance that really sticks in my mind, and which I still dance in the kitchen given half a chance, was the "Pat-a-cake Polka". We sang the movements needed (e.g. patting opposite hands) along to the music like this:

Brian Blake conducts the choir at the official opening of Peterhouse Junior School in 1951. They are singing "Autumn" by Arthur Beynon.

Left This pretty set of knees belongs to excited children waiting for Princess Margaret to arrive at Horsham St Faith in July 1956.

Right But I wasn't doing anything! A look of surprise on this little chap's face in a classroom at St John's Roman Catholic School, Norwich, October 1968.

Heel and toe and heel and toe,
A-one and two and three and four; *(twice)*
Pat – pat – pat, and pat – pat – pat,
Together, gether, gether,
And knees, knees, knees;
Round and round and round we go,
And that's the Pat–a–cake Polka!

One memorable year saw us go to the much bigger primary school in 'the village' (Terrington St Clements) to join their pupils in a country dancing day – all those children "heel and toe-ing" together, almost in time, was a sight to behold!

The highlight of every school year at 'the Marsh school', was the annual Christmas performance and prize giving – and the fundraising to pay for the books presented to us. In November there would be an evening of fun with stalls run by the older pupils (everyone wanted to be in charge of the bagatelle board, which was a bit like a non-electric pinball machine), refreshments and bingo. Then would follow weeks of rehearsals for the performance. As a confident child with good reading abilities I was often the narrator, much to my disgust!

One year I got to be Gretel to Kevin Steele's Hansel, causing much hilarity when, as required by the script, I leapt into his arms for safety from

Left Last one to the photographer's a rotten egg! It was duffel coat weather in 1967 for these South Wootton Infant School children on their very first day at school.

Right The final day's class at All Saint's School, King's Lynn, before it closed its doors forever in May 1974.

the wolf howling backstage and, in my enthusiasm, knocked him completely over! Another year we based our play on a Russian folk song learned in our weekly BBC radio programme, Singing Together, *which was called Kalinka. I don't remember the story but I remember painting background characters on large paper sacks. My mother also faithfully preserved some reports of these performances from the local newspaper, which I have even now.*

The performance was followed by the prize giving, during which each child would receive a book from the managers of the school. These were not awarded according to merit, but simply as something for the child to enjoy. I have some of these still. There was The Oeld Man and the Bird, *my ITA book (Initial Teaching Alphabet), and I received a dictionary, a Trumpton book, a* Big Book of Do You Know? *and, reflecting the twin passions of a nine-year-old,* Jill Has Two Ponies *and* The How, Why and Where book of Ballet. *Each book had a beautiful bookplate with "Presented To" and the owner's name.*

My time at Terrington Marsh County Primary School ended in 1973, a year before I was due to move up to 'the big school', as my Mum remarried

and we moved to West Winch. Although still a village near King's Lynn, it was like moving to a different country for me! The school was huge, with two classes for each year group; the children spoke in accents other than broad Norfolk and, to cap it all, the teacher failed to put me in the top group with the clever children! A big shock to a child top of her small school to be merely average in the new school! It was the end of an era for me – and the beginning of another, of course!

Margaret Haley continues her look at junior schooldays.

School outings

These were usually at the end of the school year in June and July. The annual Royal Norfolk Show was for older juniors. Sometimes whole coachloads would wait until 8pm while a "lost" child was found. It usually rained, but there were lovely bags of free handouts and super fun-packed lunch breaks.

A favourite was the wildlife park at Witchingham. Gift shops were expensive but children loved taking home souvenirs. A trip on the Broads ended up in Wroxham for fish and chips in a proper hotel-restaurant by the river. Usually the whole class (or year) was on the boat. It was quite dull as the animals were usually hidden in the reeds, but nevertheless the children enjoyed it because they had a day off school! Trips to the Norwich Puppet Theatre, the Castle Museum and Strangers' Hall were also enjoyable.

There were not many outings outside school hours. There was, however, a residential, Monday to Friday, at Trimingham. This was for 4th years, either boys or girls only. The deputy head used to organise it; one female member of staff went too and they enjoyed the trip. Children were hosed down with cold water at night and the cooking was basic.

Travelling players, who performed educational-slanted plays, used to visit schools. This was an excuse for the children to get out of lessons!

Health

A nurse tested eyes once a year. Children were sent in groups of 12 to a small office near the head's room. Those sitting on the floor waiting were often able to learn the letters on the card before their test!

Another head teacher would often read out his favourite poem – "The Joy of the Boy". Children enjoyed staff idiosyncrasies but did not show actual disrespect to teachers. They would take the "mickey" amongst themselves and only a privileged member of staff would be made aware! To gain such knowledge was indeed a compliment and showed trust.

Left The children let off steam at breaktime at Hainford School, spring 1961.

Right Boys and girls sit mesmerised at the funfair. But what has got them under its spell?

A teacher was sent to the bank in St Benedict's Street, Norwich, on a bike to collect the staff salary for Wensum View Junior School. Staff were summoned to Miss Bebee's room to be paid per calendar month. In 1947 mine was £16 a month. It rose to £10 a week in the early 1950s.

A little girl used to arrive at school every day with a different pair of specs. I later found out that her grandfather had brought a box full of specs at a jumble sale. She was not a very bright child and thought that at least she looked academic. The "nit nurse" used to arrive if there was a red alert. If a child was caught itching in class, it was very shameful for the child, who was sent home with a note and a smelly tube of "gunge". There were also medical inspections by the school doctor. A day before inspection, children were recommended to have a bath and clean underwear. (There was an ongoing fear of the medical profession.)

If the odd little girl was very clingy and quiet, it often meant that child abuse was going on at home. In my experience there were several cases of this.

Sports days

Sports days brought a nice feeling for the children because they heralded the start of a long school summer, but they were rather boring for teachers. They were at the end of the year and parents were also invited. The whole school had to take out a chair each to put on the field. Each child competed for their team colour – red, blue, yellow or green. This was a good idea because it bonded the older and younger children together. Trials prior to sports afternoon were held. Each class competed to produce the best competitors. The best runners went in flat races. The lesser skilled per class were not ignored – they went in races such as the sack race, wheelbarrow race and egg-and-spoon race.

At the end was a parents' race with appropriate awards such as chocolates or a bottle of wine for fathers. There was also a teachers' race, which was popular with the children. A male member of staff was a VIP as he had the starting pistol. He usually acted like John Wayne – such is the nature of men schoolteachers, being very important! Parents were sometimes aggressive over their offspring's rights and questioned umpire decisions. Sports day was good – the less able had a chance to shine. There was a school tuck stall that sold crisps etc and an ice-cream van was invited to trade.

"Hubble, bubble, toil and trouble," cackles this pretty little witch at the King's Lynn Howard School Christmas panto in 1972.

Traditional playground games

The hoop proved popular in Earlham Hall School playground in 1951.

Oranges and lemons

This game is played to a popular rhyme which features bells around central London:

"Oranges and Lemons," say the bells of
St Clements,
"You owe me five farthings," say the bells of
St Martins,
"When will you pay me?" say the bells of
Old Bailey,
"I do not know," says the great bell of Bow.
Here comes a candle to light you to bed,
And here comes a chopper to chop off your
HEAD!

Two children decide (in secret) who is "oranges" and who is "lemons" and then form an arch with both hands. The rest of the children dance (or run) through the arch while singing the rhyme. When they sing "Chop off your HEAD!" the arch is dropped to capture a child. The "victim" has to choose oranges or lemons (again in secret, whispering) and stands behind the appropriate child. The game continues until everyone is caught and two lines are formed behind the original pair of children. It finishes with a tug-of-war, everyone holding on to the waist of the child in front.

British Bulldog

This game can be a bit rough and many bruises and grazed knees have been sustained! In fact it is banned in most playgrounds.

Pairs of children "piggyback", usually the smaller and lighter climbs on the other's back. The game is played across the width of the playground with "safe" zones marked out at either end. One pair is "it" and challenges another pair to get across the playground. The pair who are "it" may use any means except actually holding on with hands to prevent the challengers from getting across. If they are brought down they join the first pair in the centre, making two pairs to prevent crossings, and so on.

If a pair succeeds in getting across they are safe and everyone else starts to cross, and the catchers have to see how many of them they can bring down. The game usually ends with the first casualty!

What's the time Mr Wolf?

This can be a raucous game, with an older child or sometimes an adult as the "wolf." The wolf walks slowly down the length of the playground with the rest of the children following behind, chanting: "What's the time Mr. Wolf?" The wolf replies:

"One o'clock" or any other time he chooses, and they carry on across the playground.

The children continue to ask the time until the wolf cries: "DINNERTIME!" and chases the children. They run away yelling and screaming.

Jacks or fivestones

This is one of the oldest recorded games. Sets of knucklebones have been found at prehistoric sites, and the Romans had beautifully-crafted ceramic fivestones. Modern jacks are made of lightweight metal alloy, with six "arms" arranged at right-angles so that no matter how they land, three legs are on the ground and the jack is relatively easy to pick up. The game can be played with or without a small rubber ball.

A set of five jacks is used and the game starts by tossing them into the air and attempting to catch them on the back of the same hand. Those that are caught are thrown up off the back of the hand to be caught in the palm. Any that are caught this time are deemed to have been picked up. The game continues with the jacks which were dropped. The fallen jacks are picked up with one hand whilst one of the jacks which was caught previously is thrown into the air with the same hand. (If none of the jacks are caught, the play passes to the next child.) The jacks on the ground are picked up in singles, pairs, three-and-one and all four together, with the jacks on the ground being flicked into position whilst another jack is tossed in the air. If any jacks are dropped, the play passes on.

If a ball is used, it takes the place of the jack that is tossed up whilst picking up fallen jacks. The ball is usually allowed to bounce once before being caught. This version makes an easier game, suitable for younger players.

Left Ouch! The little girl watching this duel winces as conker strikes conker.

Right Brenda Ayres, nee Germany, catches the ball at Northwold Primary School in 1957. Among the other children in the picture are Susan Hardy, Pauline Penny, Brenda Wadey, Yvonne Dawe, Michael Moore and Victor Jackson.

Windswept children wait to go back into the warm at North Lynn Primary School in 1953.

Hopscotch

The hopscotch grid is chalked out on the playground. Squares need to be big enough to accommodate a foot with plenty of room to spare. There is one square at the bottom, then two together, then one, then two and so on up to 10 in total. They are numbered from the bottom: 1, 2 and 3, 4, 5 and 6, 7, 8 and 9, then10.

Each player requires a small, flat stone. Taking it in turns, the children stand below the number 1 square and throw their stone to land in square 1. It must land entirely within the square. On a line, or even touching a line, counts as out. If the stone is in the correct square, the thrower then hops in single squares and jumps in pairs of squares, with one foot in each as far as number 10. The player then turns and hops and jumps back again, pausing to pick up the stone without touching the ground with the other foot, if on a hop, or the free hand. You are out if you tread on a line or hop into, or even touch, the square with your stone in.

In the next rounds the stones are thrown into number 2, then 3 and so on; the higher numbers are harder to hit. Once one of the players completes all 10 numbers, he or she may write their initials in any square they choose and only they may then step in it. When several of the squares have numbers in them the game becomes quite difficult.

Marbles

A smooth area is required for marbles. If it is played on a playing field a small hole is made, otherwise a circle can be chalked on the playground. The marbles are scattered randomly around the playing area. Each player uses a large marble, known as a shooter, to try to knock the other marbles into the hole.

Players take turns shooting, and if a player knocks a marble into the hole, they get to keep that marble and shoot again.

There are a couple of methods for shooting the marble. The marble can be pinched between the thumb and upper part of the forefinger, but usually the style is to push out the marble from a curled index finger with the thumbnail portion of the thumb, rather like flipping a coin.

Skipping games

Salt and mustard Two people turn the rope and several jumpers skip at the same time. The players jump over the revolving rope, chanting repeatedly "salt, mustard, vinegar, pepper." Each time they say "pepper" the rope gets faster. As people fail to jump the rope they have to stop jumping; the last one in is the winner.

Another popular skipping game was ***Jelly on a plate***. There were two turners and they would start with the rope fairly short. As they turned, they let the rope get longer and more jumpers would run in to see how many people could be squeezed in.

Jelly on a plate
Jelly on a plate
Wibble wobble wibble wobble
Jelly on a plate
Pickles in a jar
Pickles in a jar
Ooh, ah, ooh, ah,
Pickles in a jar
Sausage in a pan
Sausage in a pan
Turn it over, turn it over
Sausage in a pan.

Well, who are you then? Inquisitive children at Hopton School stop to stare, March 1957.

School survey

Left Girls skipping during playtime at Cromer Primary School in July 1962. A bit of rough and tumble is going on in the background!

Right Playtime at Thorpe Hamlet Junior School. The boy in the centre is playing on a 'snail'.

Eric Read was a youth worker who went late into teaching. Trained at Keswick Hall, Norwich, he taught in the 60s and 70s in secondary schools in Norfolk.

I taught English, arithmetic and mathematics. There is a difference between arithmetic and maths! I would leave home at 7.45 and arrive at my school at 8.15. Three-quarters of an hour preparation and into the day. Religious assembly was first. I always remember there were two little girls of other denominations who couldn't go into the hall.

There was a 15-minute break in the morning for pupils to let off steam. You could let them out without any worries. They used to chase about; boys would kick a ball around but nothing like they did 20 years earlier.

My classroom was old-fashioned. The desks all faced the front in pairs, so when you walked around the classroom no one was gazing at you because they were all facing the front. They called me Mr Read or Sir. There was no graffiti on my desks. I was "chalk 'n' talk", no handouts.

I had a chart on the wall. When they came up from the junior school I listed all their names down the side and tasks across the top. The first thing they had to do was write their name: some couldn't! If they did, they got a tick under that heading on the chart. Then their address: some of them didn't know where they lived! Then they had to know the alphabet: another tick.

Some were lacking in fine motor skills so I would jumble up a load of straws and they had to withdraw one without disturbing the others.

It was all about motivation. It didn't knock them back, make them feel unloved or unwanted. It had the opposite effect: it spurred them on. They wanted to be up there with the others. And on sports days, it was very, very competitive. Nobody worried about the fact they had lost.

I ran clubs in the lunch hour: chess, draughts and training for the Duke of Edinburgh's Award and the St John Ambulance and Life Saving Society awards.

I was also responsible for first aid and health and safety. I had a full life: the dedicated teacher did much more than simply working Monday to Friday.

Again, it was all about motivation. They didn't realise it, but when they came to chess and draughts they were learning how to reason and work things out. Monopoly helped with maths and arithmetic.

I had no problem with discipline as they were all very well-behaved. The parents were no bother; they were very receptive.

The rot started to set in when some young teachers came in. They were improperly dressed: one had a red woolly cardigan with the sleeves rolled up! It was: Don't call me sir; call me Tom, Dick, Harry or whatever it was.

I preferred single-sex schools and classes. Boys didn't show off and girls didn't become coquettish.

The survey

In the summer of 1962, as part of his teacher training, Eric Read conducted an investigation into the leisure activities of Norfolk's upper junior school children. He surveyed 240 children in the city and the county with an average age of 10½ years. The photographs on the following pages were taken by Eric at the time and show social interaction between the children. Many of the activities would not be allowed in these days of litigation.

Above Children keep their distance to allow a cricket match to take place at the George White School in Norwich.

Right Full use is made of the climbing frames at Blofield Primary School.

Eric wrote: "Leisure time activities and interests are very important to children in that they ease the learning process and also prepare them for the adult world. Teachers can make good use of the child's leisure time interests in the psychology applied to the classroom where difficulties in the individual may arise due to environment."

The study showed a direct link between educational opportunity of the child and its background. Most of the A stream children had fathers who were professionals or skilled tradesmen.

Even in 1962 there was controversy over working mothers and "latch-key" children. However, only around a third of mothers worked and all the children surveyed said they were not on their own when they arrived home after school.

Where children lived and their parents'

Left A lunchtime gossip together with knitting and embroidery at Cawston Primary School.

Below To retrieve conkers, a combined effort is required by these boys from Swardeston Primary School.

occupations had no direct influence on what children did in their spare time. The majority did no extra studies such as music, with television getting the blame.

Most families had a television. Out of the 240 children surveyed, only 18 were without one and they expressed a hope that "Dad will get one soon."

Unsurprisingly, the majority of children watched television every evening. Bedtime on a school night was around 8.30pm but at weekends children stayed up late, sometimes until midnight, watching the box. The most popular programmes were westerns, with *Bronco Lane* easily topping the list; second was *Laramie* followed closely by *Bonanza*.

Television programme preference

Programme	Votes
Westerns	
Bronco Lane	60
Laramie	25
Bonanza	24
Wagon Train	15
Lone Ranger	8
Wells Fargo	8
Cimarron City	8
Tenderfoot	2
Rawhide	1
Thrillers	
Z-Cars	111
77 Sunset Strip	16
No Hiding Place	15
Top Secret	4
Perry Mason	2
Four Just Men	1
Maigret	1
Interpol	0
Serials	
Coronation Street	82
Compact	29
Emergency Ward 10	17
Big Pull	1
Childrens'	
Mr Ed	33
Robin Hood	18
Just Dennis	13
Wm Tell	8
Crackerjack	4
Whirly Birds	4
Blue Peter	3
Just William	2
Rin Tin Tin	2
Billy Bunter	1
Bonehead	1
G. Halliday	1
Jungle Boy	1
R. Lionheart	1
Miscellaneous	
Sport	27
Rag Trade	26
Huckleberry Hound	25
Dr Kildare	17
Flintstones	12
Steptoe and Son	9
Popeye	8
Top Cat	8
Dr Findlay	5
Zoo Time	5
Dixon	2
Jazz Club	2
Look	2
London Palladium	2
Michael Shane	2
Army Game	1
Ben Casey	1
Bootsy, Snudge	1
Bulldog Breed	1
Discs a Gogo	1
Hurricane	1
Hugh and I	1
Never Believe It	1
Railway Roundabout	1

Other popular "hoss operas" were *Wagon Train*, *Cimarron City* and, of course, *The Lone Ranger.*

Thrillers were next in popularity and included the overall most-watched programme, *Z Cars*. Eric commented in his notes: "This is a supposedly true to life series but I would hardly suggest suitable for this age group." How times have changed!

In the battle of the soaps, *Coronation Street* was top with *Emergency Ward 10* and *Compact* runners-up. Of the purely children's programmes, the American series *Mr Ed*, involving a talking horse, came first, with *Robin Hood*, *Just Dennis* and *William Tell* close behind.

In the best of the rest

were *The Rag Trade*, sport and *Huckleberry Hound*.

In 1962 Eric Read expressed surprise that only 45 per cent of children in the towns and villages walked to school. Today this figure will almost certainly be lower; safety, traffic and school closures will have reduced it.

Out of school all the girls helped out at home, with the main chores being shopping and housework. A good proportion of the boys did nothing at all. Those who did also shopped, but a number also worked in the garden.

Generally, pocket money was given and not earned. Most children received about half a crown (two shillings and sixpence) per week, but a significant number got less than a shilling. One village lad received twelve and six, some of which he spent on cigarettes.

During school holidays, 25 per cent of children had no holiday away from home at all. Only 2 per cent went abroad, with 25 per cent of children holidaying in Norfolk. The traditional local seaside holiday was still at the forefront.

Eric Read concluded that the children of 1962 had a good living standard, both of house and immediate environment. Parents were generally hardworking and industrious, and cared for their children materially and physically. Children were growing up in a materialistic age and "accept television, pocket money and record players as their right."

He felt the spiritual side of life was "going by the wayside": two-thirds of children did not attend church. Eric believed that the Church and society needed to take action to halt the trend: "It can be seen in the current teenager where it will lead."

He quoted 17th-century philosopher John Locke who wrote: "All the plays and diversions of children should be directed towards good and useful habits or else they will introduce ill ones."

Right Playtime is in full swing at Blofield Primary School in 1962.

Boys stole drinks from shed

A 12-year-old boy and two 11-year-old boys admitted at Norwich Juvenile Court yesterday stealing six bottles of soft drink from a shed. The magistrates adjourned the case for ten weeks.

Because their jackets were bulging said Det.-Insp Edward Smith, the boy[s] were stopped in the street by P.S Richard Pitt who found that each bo[y] had two bottles of soft drinks. Th[e] inspector added that all the boys ha[d] been before the court before.

The father of two of the boys t[old] the court that if his sons were se[nt] away it would break up his home.

Announcing the decision of [the] magistrates the chairman (Mrs. E[ric] Read) said: "We don't want to br[eak] up any homes."

11 boys and girl stole fruit

Eleven boys and a girl, aged between nine and 14, appeared before a special sitting of Dereham Juvenile Court yesterday for breaking into a store at the back of the King's Arms, Dereham, and stealing fruit. They all admitted the offences which were alleged to have taken place in March and May.

Three of the boys also admitted being concerned together in stealing two mouse traps and a torch battery, worth a total of 1s. 4d. from F. W. Woolworth & Co. Ltd., at Dereham on May 12th.

Brig. K. Hervey told a 14-year-old boy he ought to know ...

Inevitably, children got into trouble. To explore what mischief they got up to, Eric attended a juvenile court. He says: "The surprising thing that I discovered was that the children come mostly from what can be loosely described as good homes – and from all the different social classes. In some cases it was due to tensions in the home, as was the case of a girl charged with stealing from a bungalow next to her own. Her mother was dead and the dad was out to work late in the evening. An older sister had a free hand so the child would come home from school to an empty house and was in need of love and affection. To bring herself to somebody's notice she resorted to stealing."

With Playstations, computers, iPods and television children today have entertainment on tap. So how did they amuse themselves before the techno age? As part of his study Eric Read observed children in the playground. On 21 March 1962 he watched a young schoolgirl named Patricia demonstrate that

Traditional school buildings were disappearing in favour of the modern design. This is Thorpe Hamlet Junior School in 1962.

There were 65 questions in Eric's survey – not all of them got the answers he expected!

What work does your father do?

Poison Officer (Prison officer)

How far from your house is the library?

Up the road.

How far from your house to the school?

Round the corner.

Which films do you prefer?

Western Westerns.

What work does your mother do?

Cleans officers.

What work does your father do?

He works in Granny.

Do you prefer indoor or outdoor games?

Yes.

an imagination is all a child needs to have fun.

The scene is the porch entrance of the George White Primary School, which overlooks the rectangular playground. Patricia is constantly moving about but purposely pauses on top of one of the two manhole covers in the playground for several seconds. She then walks over to some nearby benches and pretends to put something underneath them. Similarly she walks to another bench, but this time pretends to remove something from underneath before placing it on top. The same procedure is repeated using the other manhole cover, but this time Patricia goes over to a group of boys standing in a corner and pretends to give them something.

She quite happily carries on repeating the same routine on her own until a fellow pupil, Jennifer, arrives. After a brief, unheard conversation, Jennifer joins in with the actions so that both are now carrying an imaginary object very carefully with arms outstretched. Patricia, however, walks faster than her friend, eventually overtaking her. Jennifer says: "We are working hard," to which Patricia replies: "You can't talk to me. We are not on the same floor."

That marks the end of any conversation. Yet the girls continue their routine in the corners of the playground, with each girl becoming more and more elaborate in her actions, apparently trying to out-do the other. The boys whom they visit as part of the procedure continue to play on their own, ignoring all imaginary offerings.

After 10 minutes Eric asks Patricia: "What game are you playing?" to which she replies: "Mr Read, Kenneth, Brian and Stephen are fighting in a war. I am cooking for them and these" – she points to the benches – "are the ovens because they must have cooked food."

Eric pursues it further – "Why do you stand on the manhole covers?"

"Don't you know, Mr Read?" says Patricia. "They are the lifts. One goes up to where the ovens are and the other goes down to where the war is."

She continued to play for several more minutes until it was time to go into class.

Senior school

Welcome to King's Lynn High School. Pupils are on hand to greet guests arriving for prize giving at the Corn Exchange in 1967.

Whether we passed the 11-Plus or not, it was time to move on to a new school. A life of homework, exams and bewildering things like logarithms beckoned. We would make new friends as both our minds and bodies raced towards adulthood. With a fully stocked pencil case, a smart new uniform and stomachs churning we entered the world of secondary education.

There were more village schools 50 years ago so the school run for the juniors often consisted of a short walk. It was quite safe, so, apart from the infants, there was no need for mums and dads to escort their children. Youngsters would make their own way there, perhaps gathering conkers or picking up beechnuts on the way. And there wasn't a mass of parents waiting at the gates after school.

Secondary school was different. To get to school, bus, bike and train were necessary, but still children would travel unaccompanied. Some would cycle several miles; parents would find this unthinkable on today's traffic-congested roads.

Colin Burleigh from Dereham passed the scholarship to go to Hamond's Grammar School at Swaffham. This meant a daily trip on the train.

The train left at ten to eight so I was up before seven. I was 11 but I went on my own. There was no trouble; some of the local boys took the mickey. They called us "grammar grubs" and the Dereham High School girls got called "high school hags".

Some boys would cycle from places like Mattishall to catch the train and leave their bikes at mine rather than the station.

I turned up at the station for my first day and everybody was in their brand spanking new uniforms – except me. My brother had been to the school so my mother had kept his uniform for me to wear so I had a black and yellow striped blazer. However, the school blazer had been changed to all black with a badge on the pocket. The cap was the same, black and yellow hoops. The other boys used to roll up newspapers and thump me because I looked like a wasp.

And there was the initiation ceremony. You were put on the luggage rack and, of course, everyone had geometry sets so it wasn't long

Some very smart passengers step off the train at Great Yarmouth's Vauxhall station as part of a school trip in August 1952.

before compasses were out and you were poked in the fleshier parts of your body.

Then you were put under the seats while they jumped up and down on them. Railway seats were not efficiently cleaned; they harboured dust. You soon looked like a chimney sweep. If you survived that without moaning and groaning it never happened again. Otherwise you got another dose.

We were segregated in our own carriages. They were separate compartments; there was no corridor. And there was a carriage prefect in each compartment who was supposed to maintain law and order. There was not much bullying in those days; not physical anyway. You were more ridiculed, called nicknames. That was probably as harmful as physical bullying.

A master met us at Swaffham and we formed a crocodile and walked through the town to school.

The train was a godsend; you could do homework and crib off each other. The master always knew if you'd done it on the train, parts of it were illegible. D-day caused homework to suffer. In 1944, the trains were commandeered to take troops to join their ships so we went by bus and there was no room to spread your elbows out and write.

School started at nine with assembly. We had a break in the morning but there wasn't much to do. We had a third of a pint of milk, some would nip off for a crafty fag. If they were caught they were given lines.

The food was not brilliant. It was nearly always shepherd's pie. We must have had meat or there would have been nothing to put in the pie. Sweet was usually semolina and jam.

School finished about a quarter to three and we were escorted back to the station. Some boys would dodge into the cake shop in Station Street and buy cakes. When the American troops came over we

42 DECIMALS.

A. ADDITION.

1. 5·28 / 1·09 / ·83 / 3·16 2. 13·6 / 1·98 / 5·07 / ·32 3. ·64 / 1·09 / 3·51 / ·37 4.

B. Arrange as above and add :—

1. 8·91 + 13·28 + 1·32 + 5·06
2. 1·08 + 2·9 + 13·63 + ·59
3. ·7 + 9·28 + 21·06 + 1·68
4. 9·5 + 17·6 + 7·31 + ·01

C. SUBTRACTION.

1. 2·59 / 1·63 2. 5·08 / 2·95 3. 13·8 / 1·63

D. Arrange as above and subtract :—

1. 3·28 − 1·95 2. 15·06 − 3·72 3. 2·
4. 23·8 − 7·19 5. 37·14 − 24·91 6. 42

E. MULTIPLICATION

1. 5·28 × 7 2. 13·09 × 6 3.
4. 26·13 × 9 5. 9·97 × 11 6.
7. 15·32 × 8 8. 3·87 × 4 9.

F. DIVISION.

1. 3·72 ÷ 4 2. 21·9 ÷ 3 3.
4. 39·82 ÷ 11 5. 52·56 ÷ 9 6.
7. 115·6 ÷ 5 8. 94·4 ÷ 8 9.

G. By moving the decimal point only, write the

1. 3·96 × 10 2. 23·5 × 100 3.
4. 156·8 ÷ 10 5. 13·07 ÷ 100 6.

would be on Swaffham station when troop trains went past heading for Wendling.
They would throw sweets, chewing gum and tins of fruit out of the windows. Some of it went on the track so we used to jump down after it. The master used to make us leave it.

And he told the headmaster. At the end of assembly the head would say: "Will the Dereham train party remain behind." He then told us it was belittling to grovel in the dirt.

We were due to take our School Certificate in May 1947 but it was one of the worst winters. The Dereham–Swaffham line was blocked for five weeks so we didn't go to school. They were concerned that the whole form would flop. But all those expected to get through did.

I was disadvantaged when I first started at Hamond's. The first forms were 1a and 1b but for some reason the next were called Lower 2 and Upper 2. I was put straight in Upper 2. The first lesson I had was French. The master threw the door open, pointed at me and said: "Ouvrez la fenêtre." I hadn't a clue. He tore into me!

"How long have you been at this school?" he demanded.

I replied: "About a quarter of an hour."

Educated at Hamond's Grammar School, Swaffham, Neil Haverson takes a tongue-in-cheek look at the benefits of what he was taught and recalls the ups and downs of his schooldays.

The 11-Plus

We were taking an exam, we'd done nothing like this before. It was something called the 11-Plus. It would decide whether we went to the grammar school or the secondary modern next year.

When the results came through, life changed for ever. Those who passed were celebrating but there was disappointment for the ones who didn't make it. Some of them said they didn't want to go to the grammar school anyway. It was the parting of the ways for some friends but hey, we'd still all play football down the park.

The transition from primary school to grammar school was quite dramatic. Suddenly we were no longer treated as children. Instead of: "Neil, have you finished your milk?" it was: "Haverson! You're late, see me afterwards."

New disciplines were imposed; teachers provoked an element of fear in the raw first-former. They wore gowns, which set them apart from other

Go, number six! Norfolk County Schools Athletics Association sports day at Wellesley recreation ground in Great Yarmouth, 1957.

6

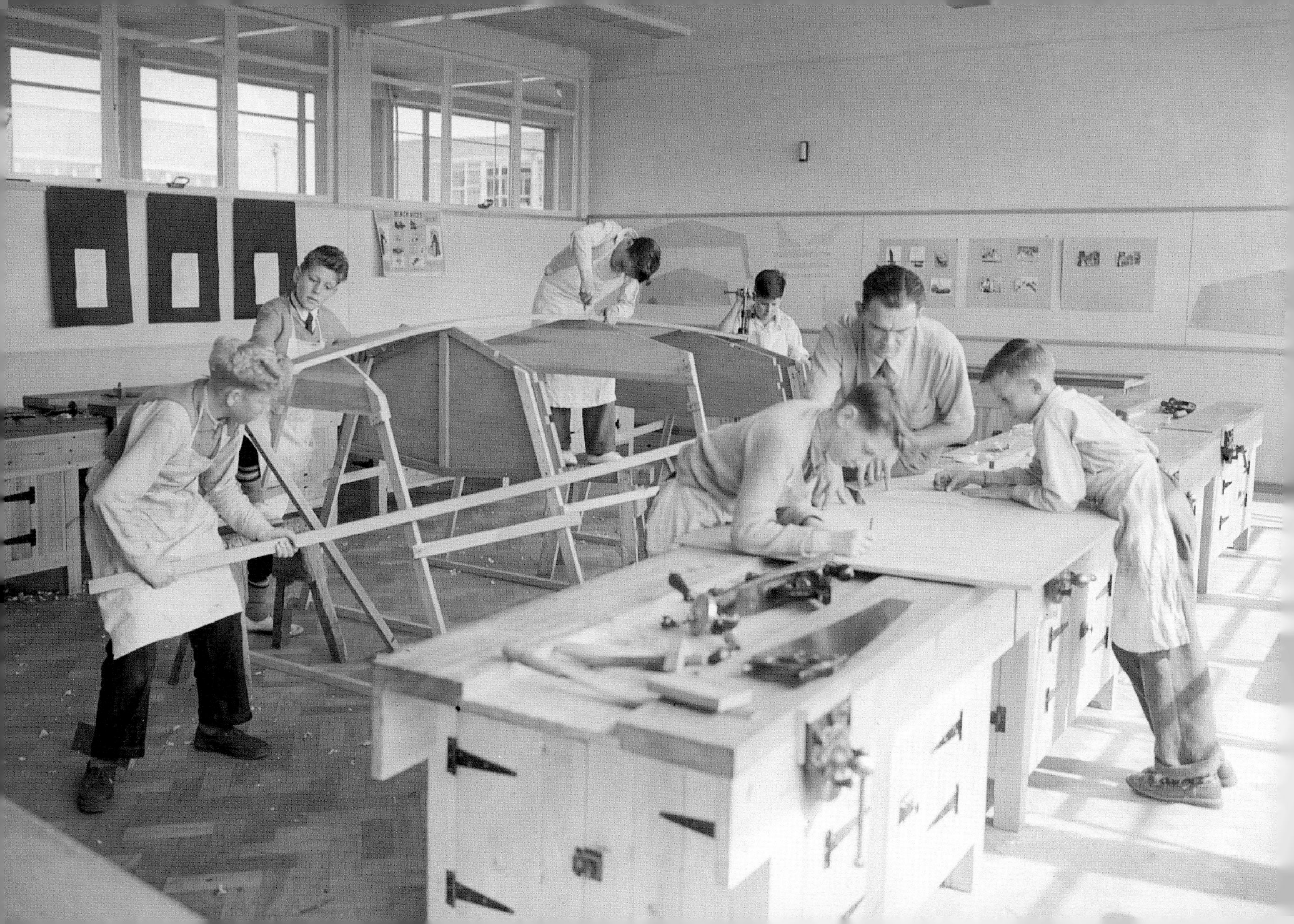

Third-year pupils who completed a practical sailing course on the Broads are making a sailing dinghy in the woodwork shop at Lakenham Secondary Modern School, 1955.

human beings. Of course, we soon learned which ones could be pushed.

We needed to learn to read and write, add up, subtract, and know the history of our country. But was everything we did really necessary?

Not once since I left school have I been asked to calculate the area of the base of a pyramid. Nor have I used logarithms – and the amoeba and I have had no contact since my biology lessons.

Yes, I know we had to learn to solve problems and have an understanding of the wonders of our planet. But I never did have the need to sit my children down and explain to them how the Davy lamp works.

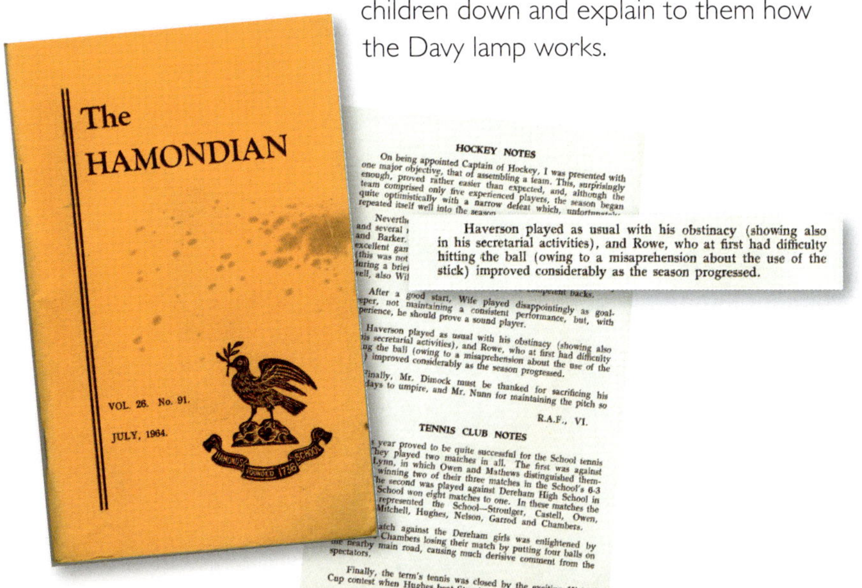

The HAMONDIAN

VOL. 26. No. 91.
JULY, 1964.

HAMONDS FOUNDED 1736 SCHOOL

HOCKEY NOTES

On being appointed Captain of Hockey, I was presented with one major objective, that of assembling a team. This, surprisingly enough, proved rather easier than expected, and, although the team comprised only five experienced players, the season began quite optimistically with a narrow defeat which, unfortunately, repeated itself well into the season

Neverth… and several … and Barker. … excellent gam… (this was not … during a brief … well, also Wil…

… competent backs.

After a good start, Wife played disappointingly as goal-…eper, not maintaining a consistent performance, but, with …perience, he should prove a sound player.

Haverson played as usual with his obstinacy (showing also …is secretarial activities), and Rowe, who at first had difficulty …ng the ball (owing to a misaprehension about the use of the …) improved considerably as the season progressed.

…inally, Mr. Dimock must be thanked for sacrificing his …days to umpire, and Mr. Nunn for maintaining the pitch so

R.A.F., VI.

TENNIS CLUB NOTES

… year proved to be quite successful for the School tennis … They played two matches in all. The first was against … Lynn, in which Owen and Mathews distinguished them… winning two of their three matches in the School's 6-3 … The second was played against Dereham High School in … School won eight matches to one. In these matches the … represented the School—Stroulger, Castell, Owen, Mitchell, Hughes, Nelson, Garrod and Chambers.

…atch against the Dereham girls was enlightened by … Chambers losing their match by putting four balls on the nearby main road, causing much derisive comment from the spectators.

Finally, the term's tennis was closed by the exciting Hick's Cup contest when Hughes beat Stroulger, G. 7-5, 6-0.

Haverson played as usual with his obstinacy (showing also in his secretarial activities), and Rowe, who at first had difficulty hitting the ball (owing to a misaprehension about the use of the stick) improved considerably as the season progressed.

I think we remember the good times, and had we any idea how little responsibility we really had, we would have enjoyed our schooldays more. Just think: no mortgage, no leaking roofs to deal with; we had parents for all that. All we did was turn up at our seat of learning each day and wait longingly for Saturday.

When I left school, got married and bought a house, geography homework seemed nowhere near as bad as spending the evening painting the kitchen. And even *I* would rather read Shakespeare than rod out a blocked drain.

But there were highs and lows of school life beyond just sitting at a desk. Here is a selection.

Football

It was Tuesday; there was a huddle around the school noticeboard. The teams for the weekend had been pinned up. Some boys turned away in delight, others looked down at their shoes in disappointment. Not everyone could be selected but it was hard when your mates were picked and you were left out.

Maybe there'd be a spare place on the minibus; perhaps you could run the line. It wouldn't be the same as pulling on the shirt and proudly trotting on to the pitch in the school colours.

Maybe someone would get injured and you'd be called into the side, score the winning goal; be the hero.

Being selected for the school team was, for many, the fulfilment of an ambition. It was just reward for all those nights on the local "rec" kicking a semi-deflated ball around. We talked about Saturday's game at break, over lunch and on the journey home from school. Come the big day it was off to school to catch the bus; the eager chatter of 11 boys as they set off to take on a rival school.

It was cold on that January day. The pitch was muddy and a mist hung over the ground. The heavy leather ball whacked you on the thigh and it stung for ages! And you lost a couple of studs out of your boots and it was hard to keep your feet.

But it was worth it. Wait until Monday when the headmaster read out the result in assembly and said your name as one of the goalscorers.

Cross-country

Why was it never a fine day for the cross-country? Off we'd go in the freezing cold, shivering in our PT vests and shorts. We wore plimsolls but no socks.

Left The cross-country gets under way at Hamond's Grammar School, Swaffham, in 1962.

Right Stitch! I have a stitch! Bressingham schoolboys limbering up before a springtime cross-country run, 1955.

Down the lane and left past the carrot field. We'd pull a carrot from the ground and crunch it, grit and all, as we ran. Right at the end of the field and past the caravan. Speed up a bit here; rumour has it that a madman lives in the dilapidated old home.

Starting to puff a bit now and I'm falling behind the rest of the field. Perhaps it's time to walk for a bit. But hang on, that fat boy from 4b is catching up; can't let him beat me.

Legs are going automatically now. Got a bit of a stitch but we're nearly there. Mind you, I'm not in

as bad a state as Inky Smith; looks as though he's come a real cropper judging by that gash in his knee.

Ah, at last! The changing room is in sight and I'm gasping for a drink.

"Don't gulp down a lot of water!" bawls the teacher. "You'll make yourselves ill."

Never mind what he says; I'm thirsty after two and a half miles of that. A nice hot shower and all I want to do is collapse.

Oh no, it's maths next!

Tuck shop

The bell went at 10.30 and half a dozen classrooms gave birth to 200 boys, most of them making for the tuck shop. Smith Crisps for 3*d*., a packet of KP nuts for 2*d*.; if you were rich you could afford the big packet for 9*d*. That meant you could keep the bag in your desk and surreptitiously sneak a handful during lessons.

Those who had brought packed lunches invariably started on them at break; sandwiches would change hands for a few pennies, chocolate marshmallows went for 6*d*.

Cricket

On the tarmac, yesterday's cricket match would resume. Two gnarled tree stumps for wickets and a seemingly endless supply of old tennis balls, necessary because they were often hit over the wall. Teams numbered anything up to 15 a side and scores ran well into the hundreds.

Why did no one take their blazer off? It severely restricted the bowling action and batting was not much easier.

And the bell always seemed to go when it was your turn to bat!

The bell

At one time the bell was rung by hand. A pupil ran past the classrooms giving the bell a healthy clang. If he didn't go as far as the biology lab they didn't know the lesson had ended until the next form, queuing outside, became restless.

When an electric bell was installed outside each classroom, crisp packets from the tuck shop were stuffed into them to silence the ring.

Assembly

Assembly, something nobody was allowed to miss. It was almost a military operation herding

The pupils of the technical high school at Gorleston assemble in 1965 to mark the retirement of headmaster Mr Parkin.

Left Engrossed young ladies enjoy some new reading material with their teacher at this Norfolk school in 1964.

Right Yes but will they catch on? Lonsdale School pupils in Norwich wear the latest high-fashion capes as an alternative to the uniform of purple gabardine raincoat and school hat, October 1971.

250 exuberant boys into the hall. The youngsters sat on mats while the older boys had chairs. There was a scramble to sit near your mates and to avoid being next to that bully out of 3b.

Hymns and prayers first; if you weren't Church of England you stood outside for this part, then filed in for the school announcements from the headmaster.

"The first eleven won by three wickets on Saturday. Somebody has taken the hammer out of the school bell. Would they kindly return it? Anybody interested in going on the trip to Cambridge should see Mr Hunt. Er…a letter will be required from your parents!"

Uniform

The uniform was a great leveller. No designer clothes to cause peer pressure. Everybody had the full set plus PT kit, house shirts for sport and whites for cricket. All parents seemed to manage to find the money.

The cap was to be worn at all times out of school. Woe betide anyone caught in the town without it on, unless they were in the sixth form. Trousers were charcoal grey. And there was that big moment when you graduated from "shorts" to "longs".

Christine Townshend, nee McDonald, attended Norwich Road Junior School in Thetford. In the early 60s she moved to the new secondary modern school which had been built in the town.

I sat the preliminary to see if I qualified for the 11-Plus. I got through that but I was on the borderline when I took the actual exam so I had another shot at it; but I didn't get through. I don't remember being devastated at the time; the secondary modern was all sparkly and new and was quite attractive compared to the dowdy old grammar school.

The first day was quite scary. At the primary school boys and girls were separate. At the secondary modern we were mixed for the first time. It was all a bit giggly! We could sit with who we liked so it tended to be two boys together and two girls together. We did all the lessons together except the girls did domestic science and the boys did woodwork. PE was separate too.

I think mixed sexes worked well.

I loved school. Mind you, I was nearly always late! I lived right opposite but always seemed to be running in at the last moment. I wasn't the most academic but I was always in the top stream at the secondary school and I probably felt happier there than struggling at the grammar school. I loved all the activities like athletics. I represented the school at the county sports. I got to the England quarterfinals in the 150 yards. I was very competitive; there was a right adrenaline rush with the excitement as you went up to the line at the start of a race. I don't think they have area sports now.

And I excelled at Scottish country dancing. Most schools did country dancing but we had a Scottish teacher, Mrs Stevenson. I liked her and seemed to have a flair for the Scottish dancing.

Left Those dreaded navy blue gym knickers! A PE class at Great Yarmouth High School in November 1974.

Right Thetford Scottish country dancing team pose for the camera with Christine MacDonald standing second from the left.

It's congratulations all round for these girls at their high school prize giving day in the 1950s. And what a lovely hat for the occasion!

Yes, we had the blue gym knickers! The boys thought they were amusing. We had wraparound skirts to go over them. There was always argy-bargy in the changing room because some girls didn't like PE and they would turn up without their gym knickers. The teachers would have none of it and had spares. No one wanted to wear them. There was a size problem; you could end up in a great big pair! And you didn't know who had worn them last!

The showers were embarrassing. We would run through them. We wrapped our towels round ourselves and kept them on as long as possible. They used to get soaking wet. You had to have a shower. The teachers wouldn't let you get away with it; they'd shove you in.

I became a prefect. We had to be there first thing for assembly to keep the kids in order while they stood in the corridor before filing in. We had to supervise mealtimes. If they misbehaved we had a word; a few had to go to the headmaster, but there really wasn't much trouble in schools back then.

We had a prefects' room where we would hang out. The head boy and head girl would give us our duties. We had to supervise detention after school, which consisted of writing lines. Something would be written on the board and they'd have to copy it out a hundred times. They used to team me up with this boy who was a prefect too. I was really horrible to him! Sometimes I didn't turn up and he'd cover for me. I didn't reciprocate! I bumped into him years later but he didn't remember.

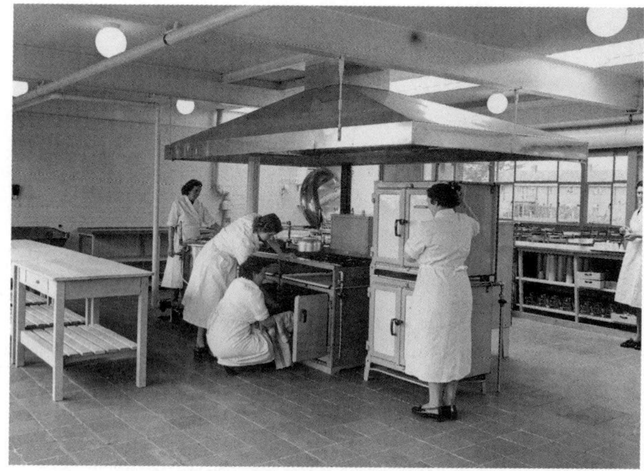

I left the secondary modern at 15 when I passed an entrance exam to go to King's Lynn Technical College. I had to leave home at 7am and walk a mile to the Market Place to catch a bus. The bus used to get a little rowdy; it was always the boys, usually smoking. The bus driver used to get upset. He'd get red in the face, stop the bus and threaten to kick us off.

We'd had a uniform at the secondary modern. In winter we wore a grey skirt, grey cardigan, white blouse and a light and dark blue striped tie. In summer we had blue dresses with white dots. At the tech it was a big escape: you wore what you liked. I bought my first pair of Levis.

I was well-behaved in the first year there but in the second year I messed about a bit. I got interested in the opposite sex! I got friendly with a girl from Hunstanton and there was lots of skiving, especially during summer. I used to sign my own sick notes. They insisted on notes or they wrote to your parents.

One day we went off with a group of boys who had a car. They took us to the beach. They said: "We'll get you back in time for your bus." But we went back via a country lane and the cows were being taken for milking and they completely blocked the road so I missed the bus. I had to phone my mum with some cock-and-bull story. I stayed with the friend at Hunstanton.

I had this big idea to be a PE teacher. I needed five O Levels; I took Cooking, Needlework, Biology, Maths and English. For cooking we learned all the basic skills and had to plan a meal – even when to do the washing up. In needlework me made a dress; there was theory too, like planning where the zips would go.

I got all five O Levels but I didn't pursue the PE idea.

Instead I got a job in Barclays Bank!

Left Something hot is coming out of the oven as canteen staff at Diss Secondary Modern School prepare for the onslaught.

Right Learning how to set a table and serve a meal in the housecraft room at the girls' school at Lakenham Secondary Modern, June 1955.

The region boasted its share of private schools such as Gresham's at Holt, Norwich School, and Langley School near Loddon. Also included was Earsham Hall School near Bungay, an imposing country mansion that is now famous for producing pine furniture, but there was a time when it was home to boys from all over the world. Derek James was a lad from Diss and recalls life at the fee-paying school.

"Come on James! Round again. No breakfast and a cold shower," shouted the man leaning up against his car in his silk dressing gown as he took another puff on his cigarette. He had watched me walking up the road that led to the school at the crack of dawn when I should have been running.

Most days there was a cross-country, three-mile run before breakfast and the sports master would follow us in his car. Then overtake us just before we returned to school – and wait. Most days I couldn't muster up the energy to run back into school so I walked. In fact I wanted to walk.

"I've got the stitch, sir," was my excuse – knowing it wouldn't cut any ice with Mr Osbourne, teacher, housemaster and chain-smoker. And, to be honest, not a bad chap. So I just nodded at him – and set off at a trot to complete the circuit again.

In fact I had no intention of running any more. I just jogged round the corner to some outbuildings where I had hidden my own cigarettes. Woody Woodbines.

Before long I was joined by my three young friends who had been walking behind me. They also suffered from the stitch. One was from South Africa, one from Iceland and the other from Cambodia. The four of us shared a cigarette and then went into an old workshop where we had our secret store of chocolate bars, "borrowed" from the tuck shop for breakfast. Wagon Wheels were our favourites.

Left Earsham Hall.

Above Earsham Hall School staff and pupils line up for the photographer in the early 1960s. Derek James is fifth from the left on the back row.

I suppose we were all aged about 13, but compared to many boys in state schools we were middle-aged men of the world. We knew how to work the system – we were survivors.

All of us had no intention of compieting another cross-country run. We knew our teacher wouldn't hang around to check that we completed the course again. He would be having his shower (a hot one) and his breakfast (a cooked one).

We were happy with our fags and chocolate – and we always avoided the showers and anyway, there was only cold water for the boys.

This was Earsham Hall School where a bunch of boys were knocked into shape to face whatever world they came from and would be returning to. It could be England, Africa, America or Asia.

So how did I end up in this extraordinary centre of education – where survival was a battle of wits? Boys against teachers; boys against prefects; boys against matron. (Not literally I must add.)

Until the school rugby team ran out on to the pitch. That was different. Pride was at stake.

"Remember, boys," our sports master told us once. "Winning is the name of the game. You may have heard people tell you it's the taking part that matters. Well, it isn't. I want you to win. If not there'll be trouble."

We didn't win all the time, but anyone who came

Life in the gym at Earsham Hall School. This was one of the postcards the school published. Derek James is standing, second right.

up against Earsham Hall in full flow knew all about it – and that included the toughest teams we played. I still remember bruising encounters at a windswept HMS Ganges.

We could hear the master, almost beside himself with rage, shouting from the touchline: "BOOT IN!" It didn't go well with the opposition – but it spurred us on.

Life at Earsham Hall could be brutal – in a way it was like a fee-paying borstal but it could also be very funny. I remember how one boy was given a warning by the headmaster for getting in a fight at local pub with some of the local lads. The headmaster didn't seem that concerned that one of his pupils, aged about 14 at the time, was brawling in a pub.

The first question he asked him was: "Did you win?" And then gave him detention.

Another boy was spotted in Bungay without his cap on and holding hands with a girl. A girl! He was given six of the stick for his "disgusting and perverted" behaviour.

That's the way it was. The law according to Earsham Hall.

So how did I end up at this place? Well, I failed my 11-Plus.

Remember that extraordinary examination that decided if you went to a grammar school or a secondary modern? I could make neither head nor tail of it so I failed and my parents decided to put their hands in their pockets and send me away to Earsham Hall. We lived at Diss so Earsham was near enough to be a weekly boarder. In a way I had the best of both worlds.

At the school there were day boys (everyone looked down on them), weekly boarders and full-time boarders. In fact some boys only went home in the summer holidays and spent the rest of the time at the school.

Back in the late 1950s Earsham had pupils from all over the world. Places that most of us had never even heard of. The strangest collection of characters you could ever imagine.

Some came from just down the road while others had arrived from all over the world. They were black Africans, white Africans, Arabs, Indians, boys from the Far East, America, Iceland. They wanted an "English" education and this came from a group of very odd teachers.

When I first arrived the headmaster was the Revd Baring – I never knew his first name – who always wore squeaky shoes.

Two teachers that stick in my mind were Major Galloway (Army) and Captain Smith (Royal Navy). Lessons were never dull when they were in the classroom.

"If there is a fire in the school," Captain Smith told us one day, "then pee on it and if that doesn't do the trick – run."

I've never forgotten those words of wisdom.

When Major Galloway was holding a class all you had to do was ask him about the war…then listen for the rest of the lesson.

Oh yes, and then there was the chaplain. There was something very creepy about him. It was alleged that he once made an inappropriate move towards one of the boys – we never saw him again. He vanished into the night. No one was very surprised.

What did I learn during my five years at Earsham? I was taught self-respect and how to respect others. I was taught how to survive. Only now do I appreciate the money that my parents spent on my education and realise how difficult it must have been for them.

And what a stroppy boy I must have been.

Today, when I remember my time at this small boarding school in the middle of nowhere during the late 1950s and early 1960s, I think to myself: "What an amazing experience." Something you could never experience in a state school.

I didn't keep in touch with any of the boys apart from my friend Richard Turner who now runs a bookshop in Sydney.

I know that one boy turned into a notorious rebel leader in Africa. One was assassinated in the Middle East and another is in prison for the rest of his life after turning to drugs and shooting a policeman.

I told you we were a strange lot.

Left The dining room at Earsham Hall School. Boys were inspected for clean hands and shoes before eating.

Right Yes, but can you do it blindfolded? Pancake Day at Gorleston School in 1951.

Eyes open please Jenkins! In this Norwich School classroom during the 1950s it's hard to tell who's concentrating and who is quietly dozing.

Exams

Why did O Levels have to be taken in June? It was a glorious evening but there was revision to do. Try concentrating on physics when you'd rather be out and about with your mates. Listen to them laughing in the street. The only relief came from a fading Radio Luxembourg on the transistor. David Jacobs playing the top 20 "brought to you by Colegate toothpaste."

Never mind; the exam isn't until 10. Always do a bit in the morning.

Then it was a sleepless night before hastening to school, a last-minute look at a textbook before filing into the school hall. The butterflies were hyperactive in your tummy as you took your seat and waited for the exam paper to be handed out.

"You may start," announced the teacher, and with trembling fingers you opened up the Geography O Level paper.

Phew, you breathed a sigh of relief. Numbers one and two were straightforward. Not so sure about three but I think I know what they want in number four.

Two hours later and it was all over and a chance to catch up with your mates.

"What did you put for number three?"

Oops, you thought, that's not what I wrote. Nevertheless you reply: "Yeah, that's what I put."

Over those agonising weeks while you wait for the results, you go over the exams again and again. By the time the day arrives you've taken all the bits you know you did right and built them up into a handsome pass.

Then the envelope drops through the letterbox. Will it be tears of joy or disappointment?

If only I'd done that extra bit of revision!

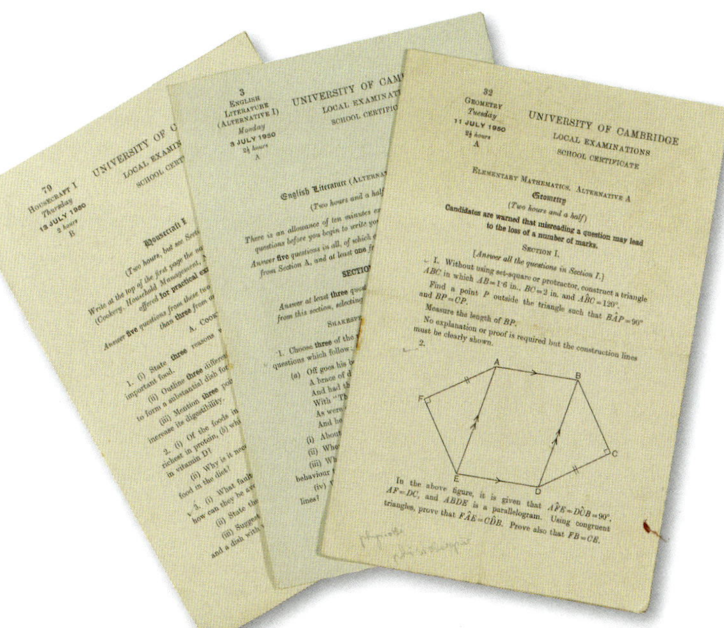

32
GEOMETRY
Tuesday
11 JULY 1950
2½ hours
A

UNIVERSITY OF CAMBRIDGE
LOCAL EXAMINATIONS
SCHOOL CERTIFICATE

ELEMENTARY MATHEMATICS, ALTERNATIVE A
Geometry
(Two hours and a half)
Candidates are warned that misreading a question may lead to the loss of a number of marks.

SECTION I.
[Answer all the questions in Section I.]

1. Without using set-square or protractor, construct a triangle ABC in which $AB = 1{\cdot}6$ in., $BC = 2$ in. and $A\hat{B}C = 120°$.

Find a point P outside the triangle such that $B\hat{A}P = 90°$ and $BP = CP$.

Measure the length of BP.

No explanation or proof is required but the construction lines must be clearly shown.

2.

In the above figure, it is given that $A\hat{F}E = D\hat{C}B = 90°$, $AF = DC$, and $ABDE$ is a parallelogram. Using congruent triangles, prove that $F\hat{A}E = C\hat{D}B$. Prove also that $FB = CE$.

There have been suggestions that current GCSE examinations are getting easier. Here is a selection of GCE questions from the 50s and 60s – see how you get on!

University of Cambridge General Certificate of Education Ordinary Level, 1963

Elementary Mathematics

Q. Divide $10\frac{1}{2}$ lb. of potatoes between two shoppers, so that one share is three quarters of the other share.

Q. The straight line AB is divided internally at C so that AC:CB = 3:5. If AC = 7cm, find AB.

Form VA. ALGEBRA. 1½ hrs. Xmas 1946

1. Write the following expressions in their simplest forms :- (i) $2p^2 \times 3p^3$ (ii) $6q^6 \div 3q^3$ (iii) $ab^2 \times a^2c^2$

Express $2(a-\frac{b}{2})(a+\frac{b}{2})$ without brackets.

2. Find the simplest factors of :-
(1) $4x^2+5x-6$
(2) $2\pi r(R+h)^2-2\pi r^2(R+h)$
(3) $ld+lt-dt-t^2$

3. Solve the equation $\frac{3x-4}{6}-\frac{2x+3}{8}=\frac{2x-7}{24}$

4. A workman's wages are s shillings per hour for h hours in the week and e shillings per hour for time in excess of h hours. Find in terms of s,h,e,p, the number of hours worked in a week when his wages total p pounds.

5. Using the formula $H=\frac{v^2}{2g}(a+\frac{4fl}{d})$ express l in terms of the other letters.

6. Find, correct to 2 places of decimals, the value of p which satisfy the equation $(2p-7)^2 = 8$.

7. 50 adults subscribe n shillings each to form a fund. Three-fifths of the fund is divided equally between 35 girls. The remaining … after a sum of 3 shillings has been deducted for … 16 boys. Each boy gets

Q. If x:y =7:3, find the ratio (x + y):y.

Q. A man's average annual salary was £620 for the years 1946–58 inclusive. In the years 1959, 1960, 1961 he earned £820, £860, £1,060 respectively. Calculate his average annual salary for the years 1946 to 1961 inclusive.

For the first ***n*** years, beginning with 1946, his salary remained unchanged at £500 per year. If these years are left out of account, his average for the remaining years until 1958 was £760. Form an equation involving ***n***, and hence calculate for how many years his salary was exactly £500 per year.

University of Cambridge Local Examinations School Certificate, 1950

General Science

Q. Define ***pressure***. Explain why a very heavy vehicle which has to be used on soft ground is equipped with caterpillar tracks.

Q. Draw a diagram to show how the prisms are arranged in prism binoculars, and indicate the path of a ray of light through the prisms. What is the advantage of using prisms instead of mirrors?

The first class to have the opportunity to take the GCE at Lakenham Boys Secondary Modern School, 1955.

Testing, testing. A class in progress at the new language laboratory at Taverham Hall School, May 1971.

Q. Define ***velocity ratio of a machine.***

Describe, with diagrams, any **one** machine which has a velocity ratio less than unity and **one** machine which has a velocity ratio greater than unity.

Q. Give an account of the preparation, in the laboratory, of a specimen of nitric acid from potassium nitrate. Draw a diagram of the apparatus you would use.

Describe what happens when diluted nitric acid is added to copper.

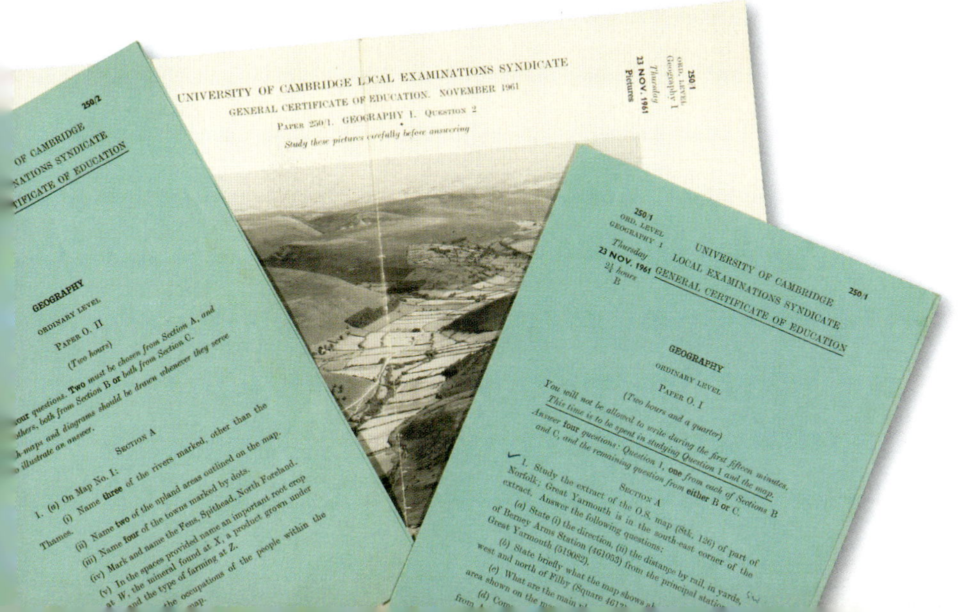

University of Cambridge Local Examinations School Certificate, 1950

English Language

Q. Write a composition on **one** of the following subjects:

1. A Sunday morning stroll in the heart of an industrial or commercial city.
2. Imagine you are a painter; describe the picture you would like to paint.
3. A morning's wait on a country railway station. Say why you were there and what you did and saw.
4. Which activities of a youth organisation do you consider essential to its success? Give your reasons and describe some of the activities in detail.
5. The advantages and disadvantages of being one of a large family.
6. Opportunities in the professions for women today.
7. Speed: its advantages and disadvantages in holiday travel.
8. "It's the little things of life, not the great things, that make life what it is." How far do you find this statement true?

Lowestoft Grammar School Local Examinations Form V, 1951

Biology

Q. Describe the part played during digestion in a named mammal by a) the stomach and b) the pancreas. (Diagrams not required)

Q. Make a fully labelled diagram of a section of the eye. Explain briefly how the eye is protected and describe what happens when you look from a distant object to a near one. (No further diagram required)

Q. What do you understand by a "reflex action"? With the aid of a diagram describe the form of the nervous arc concerned in the production of a reflex action and give **two** examples of a reflex action in man. (Diagrams essential)

Name Pamela Frost. Form IV A
Age 14y 10m. Average age of Form 15y 2m.
Position in Form 11th Number of Pupils in Form 29

Subject	Per-centage	Form Teacher	Remarks
Religious Knowledge	68	[illegible]	G: weakness in "Teachings"
English Essay and Grammar	75	[illegible]	V. Good.
English Literature	74	[illegible]	
Arithmetic	60	[illegible]	Good.
Algebra	58		
Geometry	64		
~~Physics~~ Science	—		

Q. Explain briefly the part played by living organisms in the nitrogen cycle. In what ways do manuring and rotation of crops help to maintain the fertility of cultivated land?

University of Cambridge Local Examinations School Certificate, 1949

British and European History (1688–1939)

Q. Outline the career of John Wesley and explain his importance to eighteenth-century England.

Q. Either

Describe the changes in women's dress during the period 1850–1914.

Or

Describe and explain the growth of popular sport after 1870.

Q. Describe Bismarck's domestic policy after 1871.

Q. Account for the outbreak of civil war in Spain in 1936 and describe the attitude of other European powers to this conflict.

A group of village children hard at work at Swaffham Shirehall, October 1951.

S
R

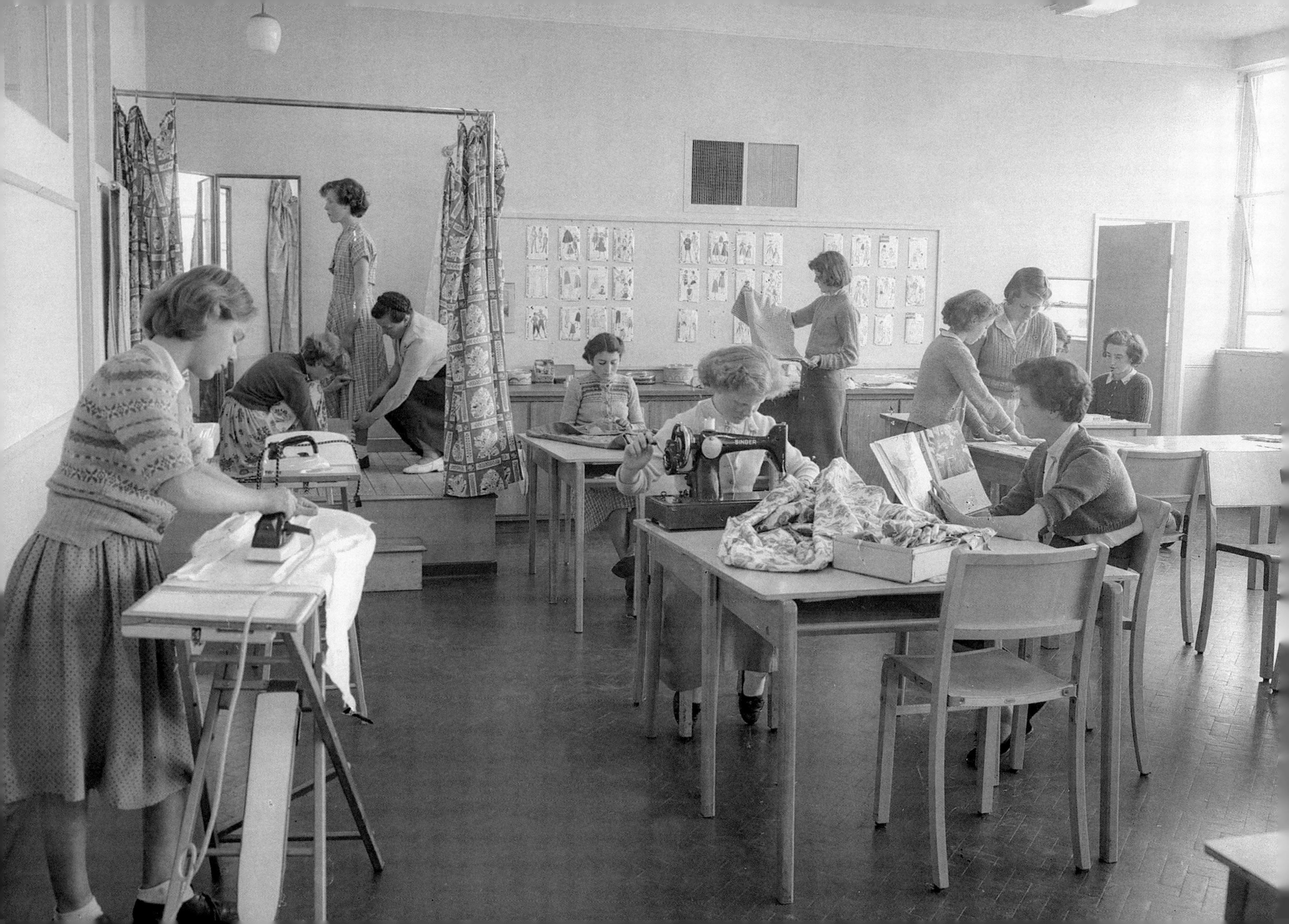
SINGER

The needlework department in the girls' school at Lakenham Secondary Modern, June 1955.

University of Cambridge Local Examinations School Certificate, 1950

Housecraft

Q. Using the materials provided, cut out the top part of the blouse to a depth of 3 in. below the armhole, for the right-hand side of the body, and also the right sleeve.

Make up to show the following processes:

a) Marking and fitting points for the sleeve. ***(These marking threads should not be removed.)***

b) The arrangement of the fulness at the front shoulder and the working of a suitable shoulder seam.

c) Working the sleeve and side seams.

d) Setting in the sleeve and neatening the armhole.

It is desirable, though not necessary, to complete each process.

Materials provided

Pattern (three pieces: half front, half back, sleeve).
1/3 yard cotton or spun rayon material, 36 in. wide.
Fine white mercerised sewing cotton.
Brightly coloured tacking cotton.

At the end of the examination, before folding up your work, sew to it firmly a label with your index number. Then place your work and the pattern in the envelope provided.

Patterns supplied by *Vogue*.

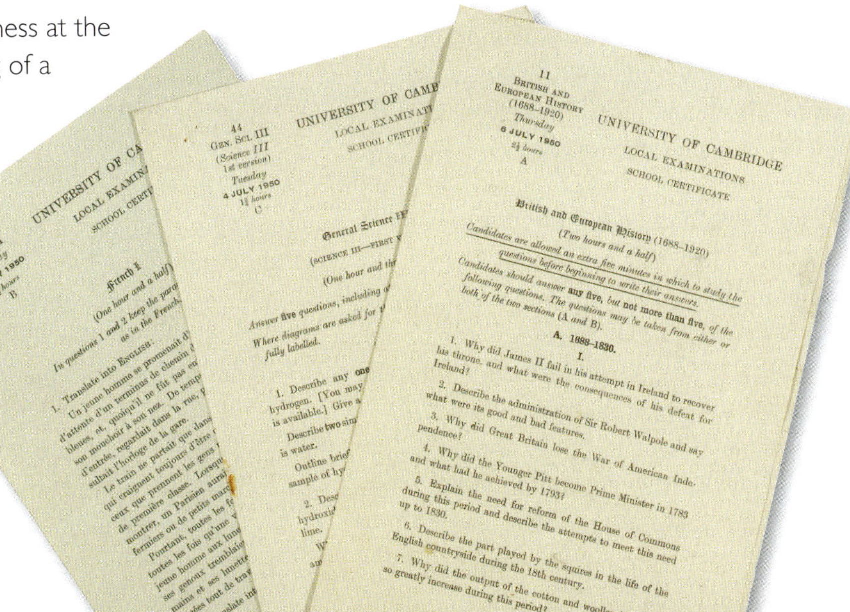

11
BRITISH AND EUROPEAN HISTORY (1688–1920)
Thursday
6 JULY 1950
2½ *hours*
A

UNIVERSITY OF CAMBRIDGE
LOCAL EXAMINATIONS
SCHOOL CERTIFICATE

British and European History (1688–1920)
(Two hours and a half)

Candidates are allowed an extra five minutes in which to study the questions before beginning to write their answers.

Candidates should answer **any five,** *but* **not more than five,** *of the following questions. The questions may be taken from either or both of the two sections (A and B).*

A. 1688–1830.

I.

1. Why did James II fail in his attempt in Ireland to recover his throne, and what were the consequences of his defeat for Ireland?

2. Describe the administration of Sir Robert Walpole and say what were its good and bad features.

3. Why did Great Britain lose the War of American Independence?

4. Why did the Younger Pitt become Prime Minister in 1783 and what had he achieved by 1793?

5. Explain the need for reform of the House of Commons during this period and describe the attempts to meet this need up to 1830.

6. Describe the part played by the squires in the life of the English countryside during the 18th century.

7. Why did the output of the cotton and woollen industries so greatly increase during this period?

Did they really say that?

Today's headlines on education talk of returning to the three "Rs", lack of discipline, modern teaching methods and the role of parents. None of this is new. A glance at what was being said as long ago as 1949 suggests little has changed.

Liberalism

Teachers should keep an eye on vitality, ability, dependability and the power to think and feel deeply enough about a cause. These should take precedence over the lesser virtues of obedience and silence. I would like one phrase cut out of the classroom: 'Stop talking'. Instead there should be: 'Talk more and talk intelligently'.
Miss M Brearley, Lecturer in Education, Birmingham University, December 1949.

The Three Rs

The National Association of Headmasters passed a resolution urging greater emphasis on the three Rs as a means of raising standards of education. Teachers are questioning if some of the playful methods of elementary education are paying fair dividends. In recent years children have become less accurate in arithmetic and their spelling and grammar has sadly deteriorated. Backwardness in reading was most noticeable, and a neat page of written work came as a pleasant surprise.
Eastern Daily Press, April 1952.

Back to essentials

The type of education today is off the beaten track. Go into many village schools and small children of six are singing: 'Sur le pont d'Avignon'. Yet by the time they are 10 or 15 they can't write their own name or speak the King's English. It is time we went back to the essentials and cut out some of the frills.
Mary Carpenter, Royal College of Midwives, January 1955.

Technology

I predict that education as we know it, reading, writing and arithmetic, will fall into disuse. The natural succession will be a concentration of radio, television and three-dimensional screening into an indexed unit for conveyance of information.

Exams at Thorpe House School were held in the gymn. Jill Riches, second left foreground, and her classmates do some last minute revision in 1961.

Town Mayor, Councillor Fredrick Page, launches the first session of the Great Yarmouth Road Accident Prevention Committee's cycling proficiency scheme in 1953. The cyclists are from Alderman Leach School.

Instead of writing and reading one will press the indexed button to reproduce the happening orally and visually.
W Huggins, Ancient Order of Foresters, September 1953.

Working mothers

There are many parents who do not fully realise the qualifications needed for real parenthood. Where there were naughty children it was often the case that the mother went out to work and was not there to meet the child after school.
Mr E H Newson, Headmaster, Pakefield Primary School, 1954.

Discipline

Nowadays we transport them to school, give them milk at 11am, lunch for next to nothing, and we carry them home at eventide. Of course they must not be caned if they misbehave; send them to a psychologist to have their 'complexes' seen to. Then we see pictures of park benches smashed and lovely trees destroyed by the products of our wonderful education.
Letter to the *Eastern Daily Press*, April 1955

Inclusion

Take 'Johnny Smith' who left school, can hardly read or write and his spelling is atrocious. When you get down to it you usually find there is some degree of abnormality in the child. In my opinion there are still far too many children in ordinary schools who ought to be in special schools.
Mr R Braund, Norwich Education Committee, April 1955.

Spending

Build a glass school and you must then spend hundreds on curtains and blinds. But you may well find the quantity of books in the carpeted library is not satisfactory. If children were made to work with reasonable correction, physically applied when necessary, in surroundings of some austerity, standards would go up. Let them sit on plain seats at plain desks in plain rooms. They will then think less of ear-rings, face powder, of drape suits and suede shoes and more in terms of what greater knowledge they can acquire.
Letter to the *Eastern Daily Press* signed "Head Master", November 1955.

In reply to "Head Master"...

In my school of under 40 pupils the cost of school meals each week is £10. 12s., the amount received from parents is £3. 2s, a deficit of £7. 10s. To this, add seven gallons of milk issued free. Yet we have no washbasins, no running water and vault-type lavatories. These lavatories have to be endured to be believed when a gale is blowing.

Letter signed 'A Village Head Mistress', November 1955.

Teacher numbers

The number of teachers is now increasing by 6,000 a year, there are many more applicants than vacancies at training colleges. Colleges can afford to be more selective than ever in their choice of students.

Sir David Eccles, Minister of Education, November 1955.

Parents and the three "Ls"

The tendency in schools nowadays is for the three Ls; listen, look and laze. The idea of work for children at school seems to be disappearing. I regret the lowering of the ethical and moral standards of parents, their almost complete lack of discipline.

The parents are handing over the tending and training of their children to teachers.

Mr D Davies, National Association of Schoolmasters, November 1956.

Left A mixture of concentration, indifference and uncomfortable chairs at school assembly.

Right Janet Pulfer, the girl high jump champion of Norfolk, being coached in hurdling in the school playground at Bressingham in 1955.

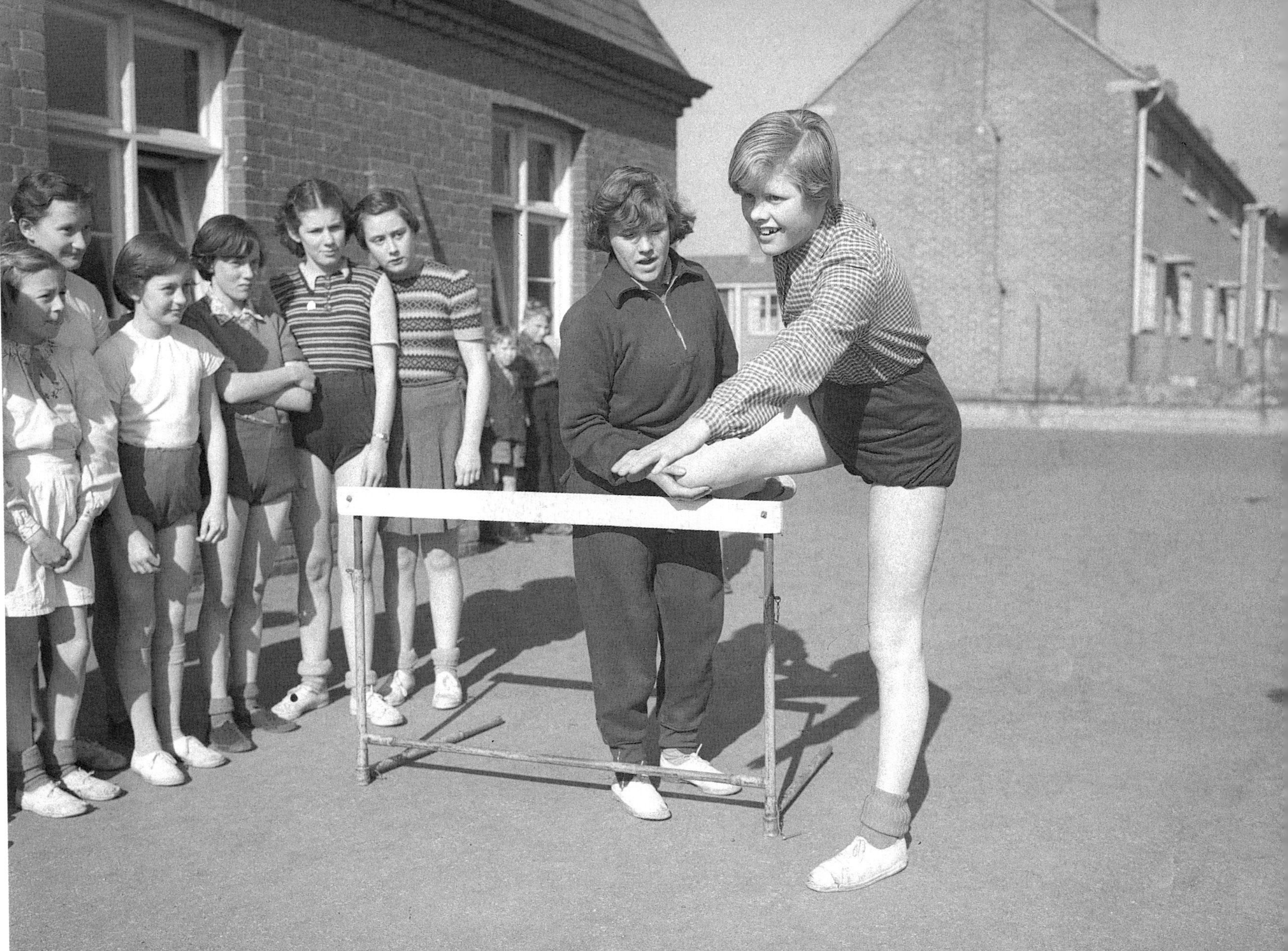

Incentives to stay on at school

A schoolmaster has made what seems a rather startling suggestion about allowances for boys to stay on at school. His proposal is that an allowance from public funds should be paid to the boys themselves! He suggests the allowance should be £1, which would solve financial strain at home and counter the attraction of the money a 16-year-old knows he can earn if does leave. If the scheme is good for boys, ought it not to apply to girls as well?

Eastern Daily Press leader, October 1960.

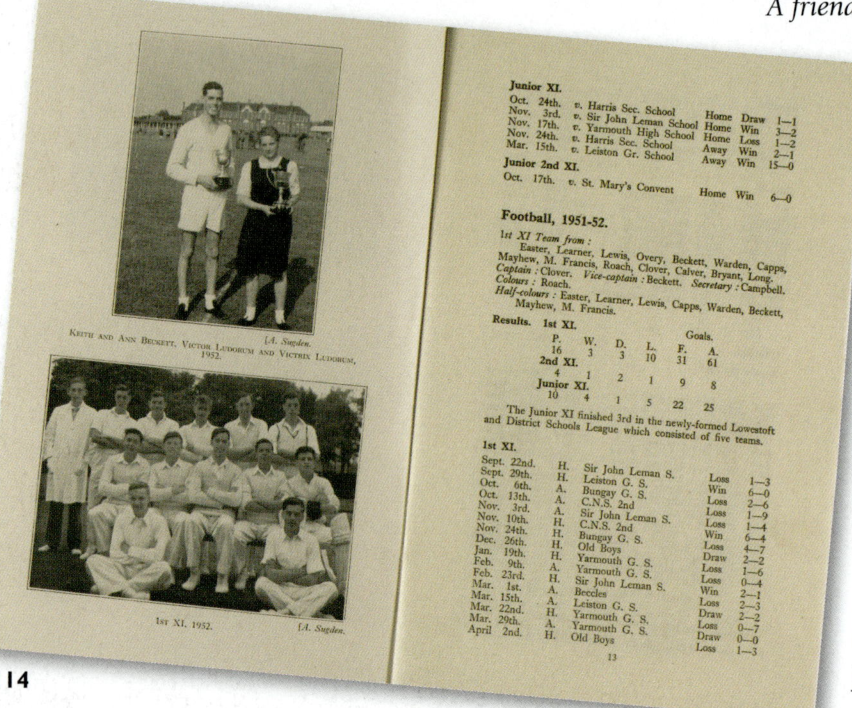

KEITH AND ANN BECKETT, VICTOR LUDORUM AND VICTRIX LUDORUM, 1952. [A. Sugden.

1ST XI, 1952. [A. Sugden.

Junior XI.

Oct. 24th.	v. Harris Sec. School	Home	Draw	1—1
Nov. 3rd.	v. Sir John Leman School	Home	Win	3—2
Nov. 17th.	v. Yarmouth High School	Home	Loss	1—2
Nov. 24th.	v. Harris Sec. School	Away	Win	2—1
Mar. 15th.	v. Leiston Gr. School	Away	Win	15—0

Junior 2nd XI.

Oct. 17th.	v. St. Mary's Convent	Home	Win	6—0

Football, 1951-52.

1st XI Team from : Easter, Learner, Lewis, Overy, Beckett, Warden, Capps, Mayhew, M. Francis, Roach, Clover, Calver, Bryant, Long.
Captain : Clover. *Vice-captain* : Beckett. *Secretary* : Campbell.
Colours : Roach.
Half-colours : Easter, Learner, Lewis, Capps, Warden, Beckett, Mayhew, M. Francis.

Results.

	P.	W.	D.	L.	Goals. F.	Goals. A.
1st XI.	16	3	3	10	31	61
2nd XI.	4	1	2	1	9	8
Junior XI.	10	4	1	5	22	25

The Junior XI finished 3rd in the newly-formed Lowestoft and District Schools League which consisted of five teams.

1st XI.

Sept. 22nd.	H.	Sir John Leman S.		
Sept. 29th.	H.	Leiston G. S.	Loss	1—3
Oct. 6th.	A.	Bungay G. S.	Win	6—0
Oct. 13th.	A.	C.N.S. 2nd	Loss	2—6
Nov. 3rd.	A.	Sir John Leman S.	Loss	1—9
Nov. 10th.	H.	C.N.S. 2nd	Loss	1—4
Nov. 24th.	H.	Bungay G. S.	Win	6—4
Dec. 26th.	H.	Old Boys	Loss	4—7
Jan. 19th.	H.	Yarmouth G. S.	Draw	2—2
Feb. 9th.	A.	Yarmouth G. S.	Loss	1—6
Feb. 23rd.	H.	Sir John Leman S.	Loss	0—4
Mar. 1st.	A.	Beccles	Win	2—1
Mar. 15th.	A.	Leiston G. S.	Loss	2—3
Mar. 22nd.	H.	Yarmouth G. S.	Draw	2—2
Mar. 29th.	A.	Yarmouth G. S.	Loss	0—7
April 2nd.	H.	Old Boys	Draw	0—0
			Loss	1—3

13

Equal opportunities

A friend was telling me her daughter wants to go to university but her father disagrees. He says a girl doesn't need educating like a boy because she is likely to marry and then her career is overlooked. I disagree. If a girl marries the wider education will enable her to put more into the business of running a home and will make her a more intelligent partner in marriage and a more enterprising mother. If she has a taste for domesticity she will retain her home skills while studying. She will probably keep her room tidy and serve delicious coffee. If a girl marries and has never used her brains she is more likely to deteriorate into a middle-aged bore.

Madge Castle writing in the *Evening News*, June 1962.

In November 1965, St James Boys School, King's Lynn, opened the first privately built covered pool in Norfolk. The headmaster paid tribute to all those parents who had helped raise funds.

Concentration etched on their faces as King's Lynn High School gets ready for a musical contribution to speech day at the Corn Exchange, 1965.

Music

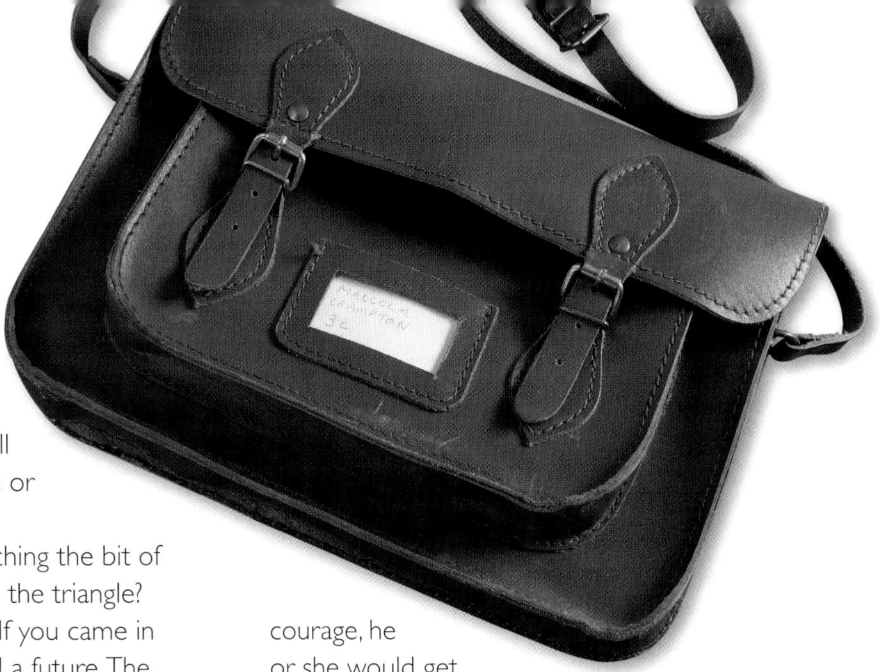

Next time you watch the *Last Night of the Proms*, take a look at the musicians and have a think how they launched their careers. Most of them will point to their early schooldays and recall those times of dinging the triangle or whacking the tambourine.

Remember standing there clutching the bit of string upon which was suspended the triangle? Waiting for the signal to strike it? If you came in on cue it probably meant you had a future. The unfortunate few who inserted the ching two seconds late would probably excel at woodwork or cooking.

If you had a flair for music you moved on to the recorder. Parents rushed out and bought us the necessary instrument and then berated us noon and night for not practising. With eager anticipation they came along to the end-of-term concert and listened proudly as the third-form recorder group launched into "London's burning" in an assortment of keys.

The school orchestra backed the Christmas carol service and played during the interval of the school play. If someone was good enough, and had the courage, he or she would get to play the piano for the hymn in morning assembly.

Joining the school choir was a good wheeze, even if you couldn't sing. Choir practice often meant missing lessons. But it could be hard work. The words had to be taken home to learn them by heart – and the teacher would watch your lips to see if you knew them.

Not many schools had their own music teacher but the authorities appointed someone to tour the schools. At one time Mr Illman would make a monthly visit to help eager young musicians. High in the hit parade at the time was Russ Conway with "Side Saddle". To conclude the lesson Mr Illman

did a fair rendition of this. "But I apologise for having all my fingers," he said, a reference to the fact that Russ had lost part of a finger in an accident with a bread slicer.

We were influenced by the music of the day. We wanted to croon like Frank Sinatra, hit the high notes like Connie Francis and play the guitar like Hank Marvin. Some persuaded their parents to buy them electric guitars or a set of drums to form a group. They played at school events and, if they were up to it, got gigs at the local hop.

For many, budding musical careers were terminated as they went through the school gate for the last time. But can we ever forget the mournful strains of the 'cello coming from the music room as someone with aspirations to join the Halle Orchestra drew the bow across the strings?

Left Lothingland School band making music in a concert, Christmas 1966.

Right Who me? No way, it was him! An accusing finger points to the player of a wrong note in the Alderman Catleugh school band, May 1974.

Left Getting down is not so easy. Great Yarmouth Technical High School girls in the gym, November 1964.

Right New school outfits which these girls from Kirkley High School, Lowestoft, designed as an alternative to the traditional uniform in November 1973.

In conclusion

It's easy to view the past through rose-tinted spectacles, and maybe we remember only the good times. But it wasn't always easy. We were at school during our most formative years, at a time when there was so much to take on board. Not only was there our education but also we were learning about life, we were being prepared for the big wide world.

We were impressionable, there were raging hormones to deal with and our fellow pupils could be cruel at times. Those awful spots that sprouted just as you were taking notice of the opposite sex and wanted to look your best, and the hair that had a mind of its own and would respond only to a serious dose of Brylcreem.

But, at times, camaraderie existed like no other. Yes there were those who sneaked on their mates but usually there was a loyalty between friends and the whole class would miss a treat because no one would own up to gassing the frogs in the biology lab.

Lasting friendships were forged and we had the energy to work and play hard. Laughter abounded; indeed we all retain a little of that mischievous schoolboy humour.

Back then, discipline was strict but it was second nature not to answer back. No one would have dreamed of striking a teacher as happens today, even in junior schools.

0 10 20 30
VOLTS

Left Pupils closely studying an experiment to show electro-magnetic induction in the science laboratory at Lakenham Secondary Modern School, summer 1955.

Right King Edward VII Grammar School forms the backdrop for this young high jumper during sports day, 1965.

The success of Friends Reunited and the strength of old school associations bear testament to the bonds that were developed during those important years. I attend the annual reunion dinner of the Old Hamondians Association. I sit with my old classmates and each year we tell the same stories, laugh at the same stunts we used to pull, and rue the day our beloved school's tradition was mothballed in favour of comprehensive education.

We take a nostalgic trip around the old place. I swear I can smell the cabbage being boiled into submission in the school kitchen. And the chemistry lab is now an IT suite but surely I can detect the aroma of gas from the Bunsen burners.

Finally, a confession: my brother also attended Hamond's Grammar School and early one term, his science exercise book containing his homework was returned to me by mistake. I shoved it on my pile and forgot about it until the end of term when we cleared our desks out to move classrooms. I remember him mentioning he had had to get a new book but I never owned up and I've felt guilty ever since in case he got into trouble.

Sorry Rod.

Neil Haverson

Acknowledgements

The publishers would like to thank all of the *Let's Talk!* readers who kindly supplied information and material to help compile this book. We would particularly like to thank:

Glenda Anderton, Bernard Brock, Colin Burleigh, Mrs T P S Cane, Tony Clarke, Malcolm Comer, Elizabeth Crouch, Emma Delf, Mr W Emms, Nigel Gardner, Margaret Haley, Juanita Hawkins, Roy Howard, Victoria Howe, Derek James, Sheila Jex, Pamela Leech, Eric Read, Christine Townshend.

We would also like to thank the staff at Roots of Gressenhall, Norfolk, for permission to photograph parts of their collection.

Copies of photographs from the *Let's Talk!* library are available to buy. For details telephone 01603 772175 or e-mail: jill.riches@archant.co.uk

Left A knight at the theatre! An ambitious school production. Could it be Robin Hood?

Right Despite the blustery weather, four records were broken at the 1966 Alderman Catleugh Boys School sports day.

Back cover The castle ruins at Eye tower is the background as these children walk happily from school – without an adult in sight.

Let's
Talk!